THE BUMPER
BOOK OF
JOKES

THE BUMPER BOOK OF JOKES

Summersdale Publishers Ltd
46 West Street
Chichester
West Sussex
PO19 1RP
UK

www.summersdale.com

Printed and bound by CPI Group (UK) Ltd, Croydon, CR0 4YY

ISBN: 978-1-78685-210-6

Substantial discounts on bulk quantities of Summersdale books are available to corporations, professional associations and other organisations. For details contact general enquiries: telephone: +44 (0) 1243 771107, fax: +44 (0) 1243 786300 or email: enquiries@summersdale.com.

THE BUMPER BOOK OF JOKES

Wisecracks, Gags and Howlers for Every Occasion

Harry Hilton

summersdale

CONTENTS

AGE

What goes up and never comes down?
Your age!

A sure sign you're getting older:
**The only thing you want for your
birthday is not to be reminded of it.**

What's the best way to get
a youthful figure?
Ask a lady her age.

Don't worry about avoiding temptation.
As you grow older, it will avoid you.

You know you're getting old when... you don't care where your spouse goes, just as long as you don't have to go along.

Age is important only if you're cheese or wine.

Seen it all, done it all, can't remember most of it.

Travelling to see historical sites isn't as much fun when many of the sites are younger than you.

Two elderly ladies had been friends since their thirties. Now in their eighties, they still get together a couple of times a week to play cards. One day they were playing gin rummy and one of them said, 'You know, we've been friends for many years and, please don't get mad, but for the life of me, I can't remember your name. Please tell me what it is.'

Her friend glared at her. She continued to glare and stare at her for at least three minutes. Finally, she said, 'How soon do you need to know?'

An elderly man was talking to his neighbour, telling him about the new hearing aid he just bought. 'It cost a fortune, but it was worth it. It works perfectly.'

'Really,' said the neighbour. 'What kind is it?'

'Ten thirty.'

THERE'S ONE GOOD THING ABOUT BALDNESS — IT'S NEAT.

My memory's not as sharp as it used to be. Also, my memory's not as sharp as it used to be.

Three elderly sisters, aged 92, 94 and 96, shared a house together. One evening, the 96-year-old sister went upstairs to take a bath. As she put her foot into the tub, she paused. Then she yelled down to the other two sisters and asked, 'Was I getting in the tub or out?'

'You silly fool,' said the 94-year-old. 'I'll come up and see.' When she got halfway up the stairs she paused. 'Was I going up the stairs or down?'

The 92-year-old sister was sitting at the kitchen table drinking a cup of tea and thought, 'I hope I never get that forgetful, knock on wood.' She shook her head and called out, 'I'll be up to help you both as soon as I see who's at the door!'

You know you are getting old when...
your back goes out more than you do.

Maybe it's true that life begins at
fifty. But everything else starts to
wear out, fall out, or spread out.

There are three signs of old age.
The first is your loss of memory.
I forget the other two.

Middle age is when work is a lot less
fun – and fun is a lot more work.

THE OLDER I GET, THE EARLIER IT GETS LATE.

gracefully is like the
vay of saying you're
slowly looking worse.

Two elderly women were eating
breakfast in a restaurant one
morning. Ethel noticed something
funny about Mabel's ear and she
said, 'Mabel, did you know you've
got a suppository in your left ear?'
Mabel answered, 'I have?
A suppository?' She pulled it
out and stared at it. Then she
said, 'Ethel, I'm glad you saw
this thing. Now I think I know
where my hearing aid is.'

Percy, an 82-year-old man, went to the doctor to get a physical. A few days later, the doctor saw Percy walking down the street with a gorgeous young lady on his arm. A couple of days later, the doctor spoke to Percy and said, 'You're really doing great, aren't you?'

Percy replied, 'Just doing what you said, Doctor: get a hot mamma and be cheerful.'

The doctor responded, 'I didn't say that. I said, You've got a heart murmur. Be careful.'

You know you are old when you speed because you don't want to forget where you're going.

You know you are old when... you look down at your watch three consecutive times and still don't know what time it is.

You know you're getting old when... it takes longer to rest than it did to get tired.

You know you're into middle age when... you realise that caution is the only thing you care to exercise.

You know you are old when... the twinkle in your eye is only the reflection of the sun on your bifocals.

ALCOHOL

Alcohol does not make you fat.
**It makes you lean... against tables,
chairs, walls, floors and ugly people.**

Alcohol doesn't solve any problems.
But then again, neither does milk.

Getting drunk at the pub
is not the answer.
**Unless you're asking what
I'm doing this weekend.**

They say a lot of people die because of
alcohol, but they don't realise how many
people are also born because of it.

MY DOCTOR ASKED ME IF I DRANK TO EXCESS.

I TOLD HIM I WOULD DRINK TO ANYTHING.

A man walks into a bar and approaches the barman. 'Can I have a pint of Less, please?'

'I'm sorry, sir,' the barman replies, looking slightly puzzled, 'I've not come across that one before. Is it a spirit?'

'I've no idea,' replies the man, 'the thing is, I went to see my doctor last week and he told me that I should drink less.'

SURE, I'LL DRINK MORE WATER... IF IT'S FROZEN AND SURROUNDED BY ALCOHOL.

Did you hear about the wall that went out on the town for its birthday?
It got plastered.

I say no to alcohol – it just doesn't listen.

'Drink responsibly' means don't spill it.

In alcohol's defence, I've done some pretty stupid things while completely sober too.

Don't trust a brilliant idea unless it survives the hangover.

WHAT DID THE BARTENDER SAY
AFTER CHARLES DICKENS
ORDERED A MARTINI?

OLIVE OR TWIST?

Boy: I love you so much, I could never live without you.
Girl: Is that you or the beer talking?
Boy: It's me talking to the beer.

A pirate walks into a tavern and orders a drink. The barman looks down and says, 'Sir, did you know you have a ship's wheel in your breeches?'
The pirate replies, 'Aye, it's drivin' me nuts!'

An Irishman walks into a bar and orders three pints of Guinness, drinking them one at a time. Noticing this odd ritual, the bartender explains that the beer goes flat when poured and informs the man his beer would be much fresher if he ordered one pint at a time. The Irishman explains he began this custom with his two brothers, who have moved to America and Australia, respectively. This is their way of remembering all the time they spent drinking together. The man becomes a regular at the pub, well known for always ordering three beers at once. One day he walks in and orders only two beers. Assuming the worst, a hush falls among other patrons. When the Irishman returns to the bar to order his second round, the bartender quietly offers his condolences. The man looks confused for a moment, and then explains, 'No, everyone's fine. I gave up beer for Lent.'

What sound does a grape make
when an elephant steps on it?
None. It just lets out a little wine.

Alcohol is not in my vodkabulary.
However, I looked it up on whiskeypedia
and found out if you drink too
much of it, it's likely tequilya.

Life and beer are very similar...
chill for best results.

I'm a recovering alcoholic. Or as my
mate describes me, hungover.

A pig walks into a bar and asks for a pitcher of beer. He drinks it all then asks the bartender where the toilet is. The bartender replies, 'Down the corridor and to the left.'

Another pig walks into the bar and orders two pitchers of beer. He finishes them off and then asks where the toilet is. The bartender replies, 'Down the corridor and to the left.'

Another pig walks into the bar and orders three pitchers of beer. Finishing them off, he was just going to stand up when the bartender asks him, 'Well aren't you going to ask where the toilet is?'

The pig replies, 'No, I am going to go wee wee wee all the way home.'

ANIMALS

Two lions were strolling down a street. One turned to the other and said, 'Not many people around today are there?'

What do you call a pig that does karate?
A pork chop.

What happens when you cross
a cow with a shark?
I don't know but I wouldn't milk it.

What is a bear's favourite pasta?
Tagliateddy.

Zebra: Let's switch roles for a while.
Lion: OK, I'm game.

What animal do you look like
when you're in the bath?
A little bear.

What kind of musical
instruments do mice play?
Mouse organs.

What animal cares the
most about its posture?
Yogi bear.

What should you
call a bald teddy?
Fred bear.

WHICH ANIMAL ALWAYS COMES TOP IN EXAMS?
THE CHEETAH.

Why are polar bears
cheap to keep?
They live on ice.

Some aquatic mammals
at the zoo escaped.
It was otter chaos.

WHAT ARE SMALL, CRISP AND SQUEAKY WHEN YOU EAT THEM?
MICE KRISPIES.

What happened to the
leopard who took a bath
three times a day?
After a week he was spotless.

A FRIEND OF MINE TRIED TO ANNOY ME WITH BIRD PUNS, BUT I SOON REALISED THAT TOUCAN PLAY AT THAT GAME.

What's black and white and noisy?
A panda playing the drums.

What is a mouse's favourite game?
Hide and squeak.

What did the elephant say
to a naked man?
**How do you breathe through
something so small?**

How does a lion greet the
other animals in the field?
Pleased to eat you.

What has large antlers,
a high voice and wears white gloves?
Mickey Moose.

Why did the lion feel sick
after he'd eaten a priest?
**Because it's hard to keep a good
man down.**

What do you get when you pour
boiling water down a rabbit hole?
Hot cross bunnies.

What does the tiger say to his friends
before they go out hunting for food?
Let us prey.

On which day do lions eat people?
Chewsday.

WHAT DO YOU CALL A BIG WHITE BEAR WITH A HOLE IN HIS MIDDLE?

A POLO BEAR.

What's grey, squeaky and
hangs around in caves?
Stalagmice.

BABIES

A woman carrying a baby passed the conductor as she got on the train.

'OMG!' cried the conductor. 'That is the ugliest-looking baby I think I've ever seen.'

Shocked, the woman made her way to her seat and sat down. She said to the man next to her, 'The conductor was just extremely rude to me.'

The man replied, 'You should go and tell the driver. I'll hold your pet monkey for you.'

A toddler was throwing a tea party for her daddy. She brought him a cup of 'tea' which was just water, of course. After several cups of tea, her mum came home. Dad made her wait in the living room to watch his little princess bring him a cup of tea, because it was 'just the cutest thing'. Mum waited, and sure enough, their daughter came down the hall with a cup of tea for Daddy. She watched her husband drink it up and then said, 'You do know the only place she can reach water is the toilet?'

Mother: Why is there a strange baby in the crib?
Daughter: You told me to change the baby.

MY WIFE IS SO NEGATIVE. I REMEMBERED THE CAR SEAT, THE STROLLER, AND THE NAPPY BAG. YET ALL SHE CAN TALK ABOUT IS HOW I FORGOT THE BABY.

What's the difference between a nine-months-pregnant woman and a model?

Nothing, if the pregnant woman's partner knows what's good for him.

WHAT IS THE MOST COMMON PREGNANCY CRAVING?

FOR MEN TO BE THE ONES WHO GET PREGNANT.

My childbirth instructor says it's not pain I'll feel during labour, but pressure. Is she right?

Yes, in the same way that a tornado might be called an air current.

When will my baby move?
With any luck, right after he finishes university.

What did the manicurist call her son?
Hans.

Does pregnancy cause haemorrhoids?
Pregnancy causes anything you want to blame it for.

Our baby was born last week. When will my wife begin to feel and act normal again?
When the kid is in college.

WHAT DID THE CLOTHING MANUFACTURER CALL HER DAUGHTER?

POLLY ESTHER.

BABIES

A man was in the supermarket with his baby son, who wouldn't stop screaming. As he went around the supermarket he could be heard saying, 'Calm down, John. Calm down. Don't scream, John. Everything's going to be OK.' When he reached the checkout, a lady in the queue gestured towards the pushchair and said, 'You're doing a great job soothing little John.' The man replied, 'My baby's called Max. My name's John.'

BANKERS

A young banker decided to get his first tailor-made suit. As he tried it on, he reached down to put his hands in the pockets but to his surprise found none.

He mentioned this to the tailor who asked him, 'You're a banker, right?'

The young man answered, 'Yes, I am.'

'Well, whoever heard of a banker putting his hand in his own pocket?'

A man visits his bank manager and says, 'How do I start a small business?'

The manager replies, 'Start a large one and wait six months.'

Bankers never give up...
They just lose interest.

HOSPITALS REPORT THAT THE HEARTS OF BANKERS ARE IN STRONG DEMAND BY TRANSPLANT PATIENTS...
BECAUSE THEY'VE NEVER BEEN USED.

Why did the banker count
his money with his toes?
**So that it wouldn't slip
through his fingers.**

I went to the bank the other day and asked the cashier to check my balance, so she pushed me and asked how I felt.

A banker fell overboard from a friend's sailing boat. The friend grabbed a life jacket, held it up, not knowing if the banker could swim, and shouted, 'Can you float alone?'

'Obviously,' the banker replied, 'but this is a hell of a time to talk business.'

IF A BANKER AND A LAWYER WERE BOTH DROWNING AND YOU COULD ONLY SAVE ONE, WOULD YOU GO TO LUNCH OR READ THE PAPER?

Whenever I go near my bank
I get withdrawal symptoms.

Man: I'd like to open a
joint account please.

Cashier: OK, with whom?

Man: Whoever has
the most money.

BIRDS

Why do seagulls fly over the sea?
**Because if they flew over the
bay they would be bagels.**

WHAT HAPPENED WHEN THE OWL LOST HIS VOICE?
HE DIDN'T GIVE A HOOT.

Where do parrots get
their qualifications?
At a polytechnic.

WHY DO DUCKS FLY SOUTH? BECAUSE IT'S TOO FAR TO WALK!

How do chickens get strong?
Egg-cercise.

What did one egg say to the other egg?
Let's get crackin'!

What do you call a winged
creature that's sad?
A bluebird.

What do you call a parrot that flew away?
A polygon.

What's red and green and
jumps out of aeroplanes?
A parrot-trooper.

WHICH BIRDS SPEND ALL THEIR TIME ON THEIR KNEES?

BIRDS OF PREY.

Which bird is always out of breath?
A puffin.

What do you give a sick bird?
Tweetment.

What do owls say when it is raining?
Too wet to woo!

What kind of bird tastes fruity?
A kiwi.

Which birds steal soap from the bath?
Robber ducks.

Where do birds invest their money?
In the stork market.

When should you buy a bird?
When it's going cheep.

What did they call the canary that
flew into the pastry dish?
Tweetie Pie.

What kind of birds do you
usually find locked up?
Jailbirds.

BIRTHDAYS

Why are birthdays good for you?
Statistics show that the people who have the most live the longest.

Little Johnny was heard praying in a loud voice a week before his birthday. 'Dear God, I pray that I will get a computer game for my birthday.'

'Why are you shouting?' asked his mother. 'God isn't deaf.'

'I know,' replied Johnny, 'but Granny is.'

I LIKE BIRTHDAYS, BUT I THINK TOO MANY CAN KILL YOU.

Why did the boy feel warm
on his birthday?
Because people kept toasting him.

What has wings, a long tail, and is
wrapped in paper and ribbon?
A birthday pheasant.

Why was the birthday cake
as hard as a rock?
Because it was a marble cake.

Patient: Doctor, I get heartburn
every time I eat birthday cake.
Doctor: Next time, make sure
you take off the candles.

The worst part about being a birthday cake is when you're set on fire, and then eaten by the hero that saved you.

A husband and his wife were out shopping. 'Darling,' said the wife, 'it's my mother's birthday tomorrow. What can we buy her? I think she'd like something electric.'

'What about a chair?' suggested the husband.

Forget about the past, you can't change it.
Forget about the future, you can't predict it.
Forget about the present, I didn't get you one.

'WERE ANY FAMOUS MEN BORN ON YOUR BIRTHDAY?'
'NO, ONLY BABIES.'

Artificial intelligence is an
incredible thing. I told my computer
that today is my birthday.
It told me that I needed an upgrade.

BOSSES

According to my boss, 'sick of being here' is not a valid reason to go home sick.

THE BOSS TICKED OFF ONE OF HIS EMPLOYEES. 'I KNOW YOU WERE SKIVING YESTERDAY. YOU WERE OUT PLAYING GOLF!'

'THAT'S A LIE!' INSISTED THE EMPLOYEE. 'AND I HAVE THE FISH TO PROVE IT!'

An employee is getting to know her new colleagues when the topic of her last job comes up.

'Why did you leave that job?' asked someone. 'It was something my boss said,' she replied.

'What did he say?' the co-worker quizzed.

'You're fired.'

A TOAST TO THE BOSS — THE PERSON WHO'S EARLY WHEN YOU'RE LATE, AND LATE WHEN YOU'RE EARLY!

I asked the boss if I could get a pay rise, and he said, 'Because of the fluctuational predisposition of your position's productive capacity as juxtaposed to the industry standards, it would be monetarily injudicious to advocate an increment.'

I said, 'I don't get it.'

He said, 'That's right.'

Sam walks into his boss's office and says, 'Sir, I'll be straight with you – I know the economy isn't great, but I have over three companies after me, and I would like to respectfully ask for a pay rise.' After a few minutes of haggling the boss finally agrees to a 5 per cent rise, and Sam happily gets up to leave.

'By the way,' asks the boss, 'which three companies are after you?'

'The electric company, water company and phone company!'

A young businessman had just started his own firm. He rented a beautiful office and had it furnished with antiques. Sitting there, he saw a man come into the outer office. Hoping to look like a hot shot, the businessman picked up the phone and started to pretend he was working on a big, important business deal. He threw huge figures around and made giant commitments. Finally he hung up and asked the visitor, 'Can I help you?'

The man said, 'Yeah, I've come to activate your phone lines.'

What do your boss and a Slinky have in common?
They're both fun to watch tumble down the stairs.

The sales chief, the HR chief and the boss are on their way to lunch around the corner. They detour through an alley and stumble on a beat-up but valuable-looking brass container. The sales chief picks it up and starts cleaning it with his handkerchief. Suddenly, a genie emerges out of a curtain of purple smoke.

The genie is grateful to be set free, and offers them each a wish.

The HR chief is wide-eyed and ecstatic. She says, 'I want to be living on a beautiful beach in Jamaica with a yacht and enough money to make me happy for the rest of my life.'

Poof! She disappears.

The sales chief says, 'Wow! I want to be happily married to a wealthy supermodel with penthouses in New York, Paris and Hong Kong.'

Presto, he vanishes.

'And how about you?' asks the genie, looking at the boss.

The boss scowls and says, 'I want both those idiots back in the office by 2 p.m.'

MORAL OF THE STORY: Always let your boss speak first.

CARS

A guy walks into a shop and says, 'I'd like a petrol cap for my KIA.' The owner thinks for a few seconds and replies, 'OK, that seems like a fair trade.'

WHAT'S THE DIFFERENCE BETWEEN A BMW AND A PORCUPINE?

A PORCUPINE HAS THE PRICKS ON THE OUTSIDE.

How do you tell when a mid-engined Ferrari is warmed up?
It's on fire.

What does FIAT stand for?
Fix It Again Tomorrow.

CHILDREN IN THE BACK SEATS OF CARS CAUSE ACCIDENTS, BUT ACCIDENTS IN THE BACK SEATS OF CARS CAUSE CHILDREN.

Where do Volkswagens
go when they get old?
The Old Volks home!

What do you call a pile of kittens?
A meowntain.

WHAT HAPPENED WHEN THE CAT SWALLOWED A PENNY?
THERE WAS SOME MONEY IN THE KITTY.

What is the difference between a cat and a comma?
One has the paws before the claws, while the other has the clause before the pause.

DID YOU HEAR ABOUT
THE CAT WHO DRANK FIVE
BOWLS OF WATER?

HE SET A NEW
LAP RECORD.

One of my neighbours owns several cats. On a recent visit, she introduced them to me: 'That's Astrophe, that's Erpillar, that's Aract, that's Alogue.'
'Where on earth did you get such unusual names?' I asked.
'Oh, those are their last names,' she explained. 'Their first names are Cat.'

Why was the cat so small?
Because it only drank condensed milk.

What does a cat that lives near the beach have in common with Christmas?
Sandy Claws.

What is a cat's favourite magazine?
Good Mousekeeping.

Did you hear about the cat who swallowed a ball of wool?
She had mittens.

How do cats end a fight?
They hiss and make up.

Why did the cat wear a dress?
Because she was feline fine.

Why was the cat sitting on the computer?
To keep an eye on the mouse.

What do you feed an invisible cat?
Evaporated milk.

Nature abhors a vacuum, but
not as much as a cat does.

What happened to the cat who wanted to learn how to bark?

Curiosity killed the cat.

HOW DID A CAT TAKE FIRST PRIZE AT THE BIRD SHOW?

BY REACHING INTO THE CAGE.

Why was the sad cat in a hurry?

Because he was a Russian Blue.

WHAT IS CLEVERER THAN A TALKING CAT?

A SPELLING BEE.

Which day of the week is
a cat's favourite day?
Caturday!

What is a cat's favourite song?
'Three Blind Mice'.

What kind of cat will keep
your grass short?
A lawn meower.

What is a cat's way of keeping order?
Claw enforcement.

What do you call the cat that
was caught by the police?
The purrpetrator.

Why was the cat so grouchy?
Because he was in a bad mewd.

Why did the cat run from the tree?
Because it was afraid of the bark.

I've got a joke about a cat.
Just kitt'en.

CHILDREN

Little five-year-old Johnny was in the bathtub, and his mum was washing his hair. She said to him, 'Wow, your hair is growing so fast! You need a haircut again.'

Little Johnny replied, 'Maybe you should stop watering it so much.'

With tears in his eyes, a little boy told his teacher that only one pair of boots was left in the cloakroom and they weren't his.

The teacher searched and searched, but she couldn't find any other boots.

'Are you sure these boots aren't yours?' she asked.

'I'm sure,' the little boy sobbed. 'Mine had snow on them.'

According to children, the perfect amount of time to stay at the park is five more minutes.

I'VE GOT TWO WONDERFUL CHILDREN, AND TWO OUT OF FIVE ISN'T BAD.

Father: Aren't you first in anything at school?

Child: Yes, Dad. I'm first out when the bell rings.

A young man agreed to babysit one night so a single mother could have an evening out. At bedtime he sent the youngsters upstairs to bed and settled down to watch football. One child kept creeping down the stairs, but the young man kept sending him back to bed. At 9 p.m. the doorbell rang – it was the next-door neighbour, Mrs Brown, asking whether her son was there. The young man brusquely replied, 'No.' Just then, a little head appeared over the banister and shouted, 'I'm here, Mum, but he won't let me go home!'

CHILDREN

If you have trouble getting your children's attention, just sit down and look comfortable.

Two wrongs don't make a right – take me and your father as an example.

I told my wife I wanted our kids every other weekend and she reminded me that we're married and live together so I'd have to see them every day.

Remember, children. The best way to get a puppy for Christmas is to beg for a baby brother.

I LIVE IN CONSTANT FEAR THAT MY CHILD WILL BECOME A FAMOUS ARTIST OR PAINTER AND I WILL HAVE THROWN OUT ABOUT A MILLION POUNDS' WORTH OF HER WORK.

CHILDREN

A man is at the local swimming pool with his children, when he overhears the lifeguard shouting at his son. Turning to the boy's dad the furious lifeguard says, 'Your son was peeing in the swimming pool, and it's just not acceptable.'

'Oh, come on,' says the dad, 'all kids pee in the pool occasionally.'

The lifeguard replies, 'Not from the diving board.'

Three naughty boys were hanging out at the zoo when the zookeeper walked over and asked them their names and what they were up to.

'My name's Joe and I'm feeding peanuts to the lions,' said the first boy.

'My name's George and I'm also feeding peanuts to the lions,' said the second.

'And what's your name?' the zookeeper said to the third boy.

'Peanuts,' he replied.

After staring at her grandad's wrinkly old face, a little girl asked, 'Grandad, did God make you?'

'Yes, he did – a long time ago,' replied her grandad.

'And did he make me?'

'Yes, although that was more recently,' he explained.

The girl thought and then said, 'God's doing a much better job these days, isn't he?'

PLEASE GO AND PLAY WITH YOUR BROTHER. THAT'S THE ONLY REASON WE HAD HIM.

When I was a kid I had two friends, and they were imaginary and they would only play with each other.

CHRISTMAS

Why did the snowman call his dog Frost?
Because Frost bites.

What did Father Christmas's wife
say during a thunderstorm?
Come and look at the rain, dear.

What do tigers sing at Christmas?
'Jungle bells, jungle bells...'

Why did the turkey cross the road?
**Because he heard Christmas
was cancelled over there.**

WHAT DO ANGRY RODENTS SEND EACH OTHER FOR CHRISTMAS?

CROSS MOUSE CARDS.

What do you get if you cross a
tiger with Father Christmas?
Santa Claws.

What did the pirate say when
he dressed up as Santa?
Ho, ho, ho and a bottle of rum.

What do you get if you cross a
vampire with a snowman?
Frostbite.

How do snowmen get to work?
By icicle.

Why is Christmas like a day at work?
**You do all the work and a fat man
in a suit gets all the credit.**

What do Christmas trees do
when winter is over?
They pine a lot.

Why did the pupil do so badly in January?
**Everything gets marked down
after Christmas.**

Why did Santa's helper see the doctor?
Because he had a low 'elf' esteem.

What did Santa say to the smoker?
Please don't smoke – it's bad for my elf.

Why are Christmas trees so
bad at sewing?
They always drop their needles.

What do you get if you eat
Christmas decorations?
Tinsilitis.

What's the difference between
the Christmas alphabet and the
ordinary alphabet?
The Christmas alphabet has Noël.

I once bought my kid a set of batteries for Christmas with a note on it saying 'Toys not included'.

DID YOU HEAR THAT RUDOLPH THE RED-NOSED REINDEER NEVER WENT TO SCHOOL?

THAT'S RIGHT — HE WAS ELF TAUGHT.

My wife took our three-year-old to church for the first time. Getting impatient while waiting for the service to start, he turned to her and asked, 'What time does Jesus get here?'

What do you call Santa Claus
when he stops moving?
Santa Pause.

WHAT DO YOU GET IF YOU CROSS AN APPLE WITH A CHRISTMAS TREE?

A PINEAPPLE.

Doctor: What seems
to be the problem?

Santa: I seem to have a mince
pie stuck up my bottom!

Doctor: Well you're in luck because
I've got just the cream for that!

COLLEGE AND UNIVERSITY

A linguistics professor was lecturing to his English class one day. 'In English,' he said, 'a double negative forms a positive. In some languages, though, such as Russian, a double negative is still a negative. However, there is no language wherein a double positive can form a negative.'

A voice from the back of the room piped up: 'Yeah, right.'

Optimist: a student who opens his wallet and expects to find money.

Professor: What inspired you to write this essay?
Student: The deadline.

ON WHAT KIND OF SHIPS DO STUDENTS STUDY?

SCHOLARSHIPS.

What is the fundamental lesson you learn at university?

That you reached your academic peak at 11 years old.

I THOUGHT ABOUT STUDYING ASTRONOMY AT UNIVERSITY, BUT I KNEW I WOULD JUST BE TAKING UP SPACE.

University is where you question how on earth you were able to wake up at 7 a.m. every day in secondary school.

University is a lot like preschool. You sleep a lot, miss your mum and have no clue what's going on.

How many theatre students does it take to screw in a light bulb?
Um, what's the deadline? I may need an extension.

If you plant pasta and water it with alcohol, a university student will grow.

A college student delivered a pizza to an old man's house. 'I suppose you want a tip?' said the old man grumpily.

'That would be much appreciated,' said the student, 'but the other guy who does pizza deliveries told me not to expect much from you. He said if I got a penny from you, I'd be lucky.'

The elderly man was hurt by the accusation. 'Well, to prove him wrong, here's five pounds.'

'Thank you,' said the student, 'I'll put this in my school fund.'

'What are you studying?' asked the old man.

'Applied psychology.'

COMPUTERS

What do scientists have for a snack?
Micro-chips.

Why did the computer get cold?
Because it forgot to close Windows.

Why did the computer keep sneezing?
Because it got a virus.

There's a band called 1023 MB.
They haven't had any gigs yet.

I LOVE PRESSING F5. IT IS SO REFRESHING.

Why did the computer squeak?
**Because someone stepped
on its mouse.**

What do you get when you cross
a computer and a lifeguard?
A screensaver.

What did the spider do on the computer?
Made a website.

What did the computer do at lunchtime?
Had a byte.

WHY WAS THE COMPUTER TIRED
WHEN HE GOT HOME?

BECAUSE HE HAD A HARD DRIVE.

The lumberjack loved his new computer.
He especially enjoyed logging in.

My email password has been
hacked. That's the third time
I've had to rename the cat.

What did the computer
geek say to the girl?
**Is your name Wi-Fi? Because
I'm feeling a connection.**

A computer lets you make more
mistakes faster than any invention
in human history – with the possible
exceptions of handguns and tequila.

A helpful neighbour was in a couple's home trying to fix their internet connection. The husband called out to his wife in the other room for the computer password. 'Start with a capital S, then 123,' she shouted back. The men tried S123 several times, but it didn't work. So they called the wife in. As she input the password, she muttered, 'I really don't know what's so difficult about typing Start123.'

CRICKET

Why did Robin get
sent off the field?

Because he broke his bat, man.

Two cricket teammates were
having a pint. One said to
the other, 'What's up? You're
looking miserable.'

The other replied, 'I am. My doctor
told me I can't play cricket.'

His friend looked surprised
and said, 'I didn't know he was
at the game on Sunday.'

BATSMAN: MY WIFE SAID SHE'S GOING TO LEAVE ME IF I DON'T STOP PLAYING CRICKET.

WICKET KEEPER: OH DEAR. THAT'S TERRIBLE.

BATSMAN: YES, I SUPPOSE I'LL MISS HER.

Brian asked his boss for the afternoon off so he could go to his uncle's funeral. He actually went to a cricket match where the score was 220 for 0. Turning around he came face to face with his boss.

'So, I suppose this is your uncle's funeral,' said his boss, rather annoyed.

'Could be,' replied Brian. 'He's the bowler.'

Why do most cricketers look weather-beaten?

Because rain always stops play.

A batsman collapsed in a miserable heap in the pavilion and moaned, 'I've never played that badly before. I don't know what happened.'

His captain turned around and replied, 'Oh, you've played before, have you?'

Middlesex and Yorkshire were playing at Lords. A man with a large white rose approached the ticket office and asked the price. 'Ten pounds please, sir,' was the girl's reply.

'Well then, there's five pounds,' the man said, handing over the money. 'There's only one team worth watching.'

Doctor, doctor, I feel
like a cricket ball.
You'll soon be over that.

WHY IS IT CALLED A HAT-TRICK?
BECAUSE IT'S PERFORMED BY A BOWLER.

The Devil suggested there should
be a cricket match between
heaven and hell. 'That wouldn't
work,' said God, smiling. 'We
have all the cricketers.'

The Devil replied, 'Yes, but
we have all the umpires.'

CRIME AND PUNISHMENT

A snail was mugged in an alley by two slugs. Later a detective asked him for a description of the assailants. 'Cripes,' said the snail, 'I'm not sure – it all happened so fast.'

Why did the escaped convict saw the legs off his bed?
He wanted to lie low.

Did you hear about the thief who stole a calendar?
He got 12 months.

Judge: Why did you steal that bird?
Prisoner: For a lark, sir.

DID YOU HEAR ABOUT THE BURGLAR WHO FELL IN THE CEMENT MIXER?

NOW HE'S A HARDENED CRIMINAL.

CRIME AND PUNISHMENT

It was Christmas and the judge was in a merry mood as he asked the prisoner, 'What are you charged with?'

'Doing my Christmas shopping early,' replied the defendant.

'That's no offence,' said the judge. 'How early were you doing this shopping?'

'Before the store opened,' the prisoner confessed.

A bank robber rushed into a bank, pointed two fingers at the clerk and said, 'This is a muck up!'

'Don't you mean a stick up?' asked the girl behind the counter.

'No,' said the robber, 'it's a muck up. I've forgotten my gun.'

What diploma do criminals get?
The third degree.

WHY DID THE BURGLAR TAKE A SHOWER?

HE WANTED TO MAKE A CLEAN GETAWAY

Why did the picture go to prison?
Because it was framed.

Detective: Why did you dump those vegetables on my desk?
Criminal: You said it was time to spill the beans.

Why was the robber so secure?
He was a safe robber.

Fred: We had a burglary last night, and they took everything except the soap and towels.
Harry: The dirty crooks.

Who is the strongest thief?
A shoplifter.

A woman woke her husband in the middle of the night. 'There's a burglar downstairs eating the cake that I made this morning.'

'Who shall I call,' her husband asked, 'police or ambulance?'

WHAT WAS THE PARROT DOING IN PRISON?

IT WAS A JAILBIRD.

What did the burglar say to the watchmaker as he tied him up?

Sorry to take so much of your valuable time.

Weight loss pills stolen
this morning – police say
suspects are still at large.

I NEVER LIKED BEFRIENDING ASSASSINS — THEY'RE ALL BACKSTABBERS.

Teacher: Johnny, what do you want to be when you grow up?

Johnny: I'm gonna follow in my dad's footsteps and be a cop.

Teacher: Is your dad a cop?

Johnny: No, he's a bank robber.

DATING

A college friend was going to meet a young lady he knew.

'An old flame?' I asked.

He winked and said, 'More like an unlit match.'

Sarah: I hear you broke off your engagement to Rob. Why?

Michelle: It's just that my feelings toward him weren't the same any more.

Sarah: Are you returning his ring?

Michelle: No way! My feelings towards the ring haven't changed one bit!

He: Will you go out with me this Saturday?

She: Sorry. I am having a headache this weekend.

NINETY PER CENT OF A RELATIONSHIP IS FIGURING OUT WHERE TO EAT.

He: Can I buy you a drink?

She: I would rather have the money.

A good boyfriend will never want to change anything about you... except your last name.

DID YOU HEAR OXYGEN WENT ON A DATE WITH POTASSIUM?

IT WENT OK.

That tingly feeling you get when you meet someone you're really attracted to?

That's common sense leaving your body.

A GIRL AND HER BOYFRIEND
WENT TO A PARTY DRESSED
AS A BARCODE.

THEY WERE AN ITEM.

When a psychic showed
me the girl I'll marry, it was
love at second sight.

HELICOPTER RESCUE PILOTS HAVE THE MOST SUCCESSFUL PICK-UP LINES.

Saw a couple holding hands while
jogging and it made me hopeful
that one day I will meet someone
who will hate them with me.

A man went to the doctors for his annual physical. The man was stunned when the doctor said, 'I'm afraid you've only got six weeks to live.'

'I can't believe it,' said the man. 'I feel great – isn't there anything I can do?'

'Well you could try taking a mud bath every day.'

'Why, will that cure me?' said the man hopefully.

'No, but it'll get you used to the dirt.'

'Mum,' said the son to his ageing mother, 'when you go, do you want to be buried or cremated?'

'I don't mind,' replied the mother. 'Surprise me.'

What do you call a woman
who knows where her
husband is every night?
A widow.

DID YOU HEAR ABOUT THE MAN WHO LEFT HIS ROLE AT THE MORTUARY?
IT WAS A DEAD-END JOB.

Why did the hamster die?
He fell asleep at the wheel.

I SAW AN AD FOR BURIAL PLOTS, AND THOUGHT TO MYSELF: THIS IS THE LAST THING I NEED.

DEATH

A husband and wife were sitting at home when the husband suddenly said, 'Darling, just so you know, I never want to be kept alive in a vegetative state, dependent on some machine and fluids from a bottle. If that ever happens, just pull the plug.'

So the wife got up, pulled the plug on the TV and threw out all of his beer.

When I was younger I hated going to weddings. It seemed that all of my aunts and the grandmotherly types used to come up to me, poking me in the ribs and cackling, telling me, 'You're next.'

They stopped that after I started doing the same thing to them at funerals.

Old software engineers never die.
They just log out.

A reporter was interviewing a 103-year-old great grandfather: 'And what do you think is the best thing about being 103?' the reporter asked.
He simply replied, 'No peer pressure.'

I'll never forget my grandfather's last words: 'Stop shaking the ladder, you idiot!'

What do you do with a dead chemist?
Barium.

'I'm really worried,' says a nervous patient to his nurse. 'Last week, I read about a man who was in the hospital because of heart trouble and he died of malaria.'

'Relax,' replies the nurse. 'This is a first-rate hospital. When we treat you for heart trouble, you die of heart trouble.'

Doctor: You're in good health. You'll live to be 80.

Patient: But, doctor, I am 80 right now.

Doctor: See, what did I tell you?

DIVORCE

Why is getting divorced
so expensive?
Because it's worth it.

'Grandma, how long have
you and Grandpa been
married?' asked young Nina.
'Fifty years,' Grandma replied.
'That is so wonderful,' exclaimed
Nina. 'And I bet in all that time,
you never once thought
about divorce, right?'
'Right, Nina. Divorce, NEVER.
Murder, lots of times.'

MY HUSBAND AND I DIVORCED OVER RELIGIOUS DIFFERENCES.

HE THOUGHT HE WAS GOD AND I DIDN'T.

A young woman is divorced after only a few years of marriage, and soon afterwards her friends begin to ask her if she is thinking of marrying again.

'Right now, no,' the young woman answers. 'I've hardly begun to enjoy using the remote control.'

Two newlyweds quickly realised that the marriage wasn't working and filed for divorce. The judge wanted to know what the problem was.

The husband answered, 'In the seven weeks that we've been together, we haven't been able to agree on a single thing.'

The judge turned to the wife: 'Have you anything to say?'

She replied, 'It's been eight weeks, your honour.'

DOCTORS

'Doctor, doctor, I can't stop
my hands from shaking.'
'Do you drink a lot?'
'Not really – I spill most of it!'

'Doctor, doctor, I think I'm a dog.'
'Why don't you sit on the sofa
so we can talk about it?'
'But I'm not allowed on the sofa!'

'Doctor, doctor, I keep
thinking I'm a goat.'
'How long have you felt like this?'
'Ever since I was a kid.'

Adam, an elderly man, was seated in the doctor's waiting room. When he was called in to see the doctor, Adam slowly got up, and, grasping his cane and hunching over, slowly made his way into the examining room.

After only a few minutes, Adam emerged from the room, walking completely upright. Paul, another patient who had watched him hobble into the room all hunched over, stared in amazement. 'That must be a miracle doctor in there!' he exclaimed. 'What treatment did he give you? What's his secret?'

Adam stared at Paul and said, 'Well, the doctor looked me up and down, analysed the situation, and gave me a cane that was four inches longer than the one I had been using.'

'Doctor, doctor, I keep
seeing double.'
'Please sit on the couch.'
'Which one?'

**'DOCTOR, DOCTOR, SINCE MY
OPERATION I'VE HAD TWO HEARTBEATS.'
'AH, SO THAT'S WHERE MY
WRISTWATCH WENT!'**

'Doctor, doctor, my wife
thinks she's a goose.'
'Send her in to see me.'
'I can't – she's flown
south for the winter.'

'Doctor, doctor, you've taken out my tonsils, my gall bladder and my appendix, but I still feel ill.'
'That's quite enough out of you!'

'DOCTOR, DOCTOR, WHAT DO YOU CHARGE FOR TREATING A SPLIT PERSONALITY?'
'FIFTEEN POUNDS EACH.'

'Doctor, doctor, there's a carrot growing in my ear.'
'How did that happen?'
'I don't know – I planted cauliflowers.'

'Doctor, doctor, what do you recommend for flat feet?'

'Try a foot pump.'

'DOCTOR, DOCTOR, I NEED SOMETHING FOR MY KIDNEYS.'

'THIS ISN'T A BUTCHER'S.'

A mother complained to her consultant about her daughter's strange eating habits. 'All day long she lies in bed and eats yeast and car wax. What will happen to her?'

'Eventually,' said the consultant, 'she will rise and shine.'

'Doctor, doctor, my aunt has a sore throat.'
'Give her this bottle of auntie-septic.'

'Doctor, doctor, my mind keeps wandering.'
'Don't worry – it's too weak to go very far.'

'Doctor, doctor, I'm just not myself.'
'Yes – I noticed the improvement.'

'Doctor, doctor, I can't stop trembling.'
'I'll be with you in a couple of shakes.'

'Doctor, doctor, my daughter
thinks she's an actress.'

'Don't worry – it's just a stage
she's going through.'

**'DOCTOR, DOCTOR, WHEN I GET
UP IN THE MORNING, I'M ALWAYS
DIZZY FOR HALF AN HOUR.'**

'TRY GETTING UP HALF AN HOUR LATER.'

'Doctor, doctor, my sister
thinks she is a lift.'

'Well, tell her to come in.'

'I can't – she doesn't
stop at this floor!'

'DOCTOR, DOCTOR, I KEEP SEEING PURPLE AND YELLOW SPOTS.'

'HAVE YOU SEEN AN OPTICIAN?'

'NO — JUST PURPLE AND YELLOW SPOTS.'

'Doctor, doctor, I can't stop robbing banks.'
'Sit down and I'll take a few notes.'

Patient: Doctor, when I press my leg it hurts. Then when I press my chest it hurts, when I press my head it hurts, and when I press my stomach it hurts. I'm worried, Doc. What's wrong with me?

Doctor: That's easy, you have a sore finger!

'Doctor, doctor, I can't stop shoplifting.'
'Have you taken anything for it?'

'Doctor, doctor, I'm only four feet tall.'
'You'll just have to be a little patient.'

A woman was terribly overweight, so her doctor put her on a diet. The doctor said, 'I want you to eat regularly for two days, then skip a day, and repeat this procedure for two weeks. When the woman returned, she shocked the doctor by having lost nearly 20 pounds.

'Why, that's amazing!' the doctor said. 'Did you follow my instructions?'

The woman nodded. 'But let me tell you, I thought I was going to drop dead that third day.'

The doctor, looking somewhat puzzled, said: 'From hunger, you mean?'

'No, from skipping.'

'Doctor, doctor, I can't get to sleep.'
'Sit on the edge of the bed
and you'll soon drop off.'

'DOCTOR, DOCTOR, CAN I HAVE A SECOND OPINION?'
'OF COURSE, COME BACK TOMORROW.'

'Doctor, doctor, I can't
stop telling lies.'
'You don't expect me to
believe that, do you?'

'Doctor, doctor, I've got wind! Can
you give me something?'
'Yes – here's a kite!'

'Doctor, doctor, I've a terrible
problem. Can you help me out?'
'Certainly – which way did you come in?'

'Doctor, doctor, I've been stung by a
bee. Shall I put some ointment on it?'
'Don't be silly – it must be
miles away by now.'

'Doctor, doctor, my little boy has
just swallowed a roll of film.'
'Don't panic – call me back
if anything develops.'

'Doctor, doctor, I think I've
been bitten by a vampire.'
'Drink this glass of water.'
'Will it make me better?'
'No, but I'll be able to see
if your neck leaks.'

'DOCTOR, DOCTOR, I THINK I'M A TELEPHONE.'

'WELL, TAKE THESE PILLS AND IF THEY DON'T WORK THEN GIVE ME A RING.'

'Doctor, doctor, I'm having trouble
pronouncing F's, T's and H's.'
'Well, you can't say fairer
than that then.'

DOGS

What is a dog's favourite city?
New Yorkie.

Who is a dog's favourite comedian?
Growlcho Marx.

What do you get if you take a
really big dog out for a walk?
A Great Dane out.

What did the hungry
Dalmatian say after eating?
'That hit the spots.'

What kind of dog chases anything red?
A bulldog.

Why do dogs run in circles?
Because it's hard to run in squares.

What do baby dogs eat at the cinema?
Pupcorn.

**How do you find your dog if
he's lost in the woods?**

Put your ear to a tree and
listen for the bark.

HOW DO YOU KEEP A DOG FROM BARKING IN YOUR FRONT GARDEN?

PUT HIM IN YOUR BACK GARDEN.

If you take your dog into town,
where should you leave him?
In a barking lot.

Which dog can tell the time?
A watchdog.

What place of business helps
dogs that have lost their tails?
A retail store.

Which dog needs contact lenses?
A cock-eyed spaniel.

What did the dog do when a man-eating tiger followed him?

Nothing. It was a man-eating tiger, not a dog-eating one.

WHY DID THE DOG SLEEP ON THE CHANDELIER?

HE WAS A LIGHT SLEEPER.

Why is it called a 'litter' of puppies?

Because they mess up the whole house.

WHAT HAPPENED TO THE DOG THAT ATE NOTHING BUT GARLIC? HIS BARK WAS MUCH WORSE THAN HIS BITE.

How did the little Scottish
dog feel when he saw the
Loch Ness Monster?
Terrier-fied.

WHERE DO YOU FIND A
DOG WITH NO LEGS?
THE SAME PLACE YOU LEFT HIM.

Why aren't dogs good dancers?
Because they've got two left feet.

FAMILIES

A family is like a box of chocolates. **They're mostly sweet, with a few nuts.**

A man went to the doctor for a check-up and was told he had high blood pressure. 'It runs in the family,' he said.

'On your mother or father's side?' asked the doctor.

'Neither,' the man replied. 'It's on my wife's side.'

The doctor, confused, asked, 'How can your wife's family give you high blood pressure?'

The man replied, 'You try spending the weekend with them and you'll see.'

How do you make antifreeze?
Steal her pyjamas.

BE NICE TO YOUR KIDS. THEY'LL CHOOSE YOUR NURSING HOME.

My grandfather has the heart of a lion and a lifetime ban from the local zoo.

A TEENAGE GIRL HAD BEEN CHATTING ON THE PHONE FOR ABOUT AN HOUR BEFORE SHE HUNG UP. HER FATHER, IMPRESSED, SAID, 'THAT WAS A QUICK CHAT FOR YOU — YOU'RE USUALLY ON THAT THING FOR AT LEAST TWO HOURS.' HIS DAUGHTER SMILED AND SAID, 'OH, IT WAS A WRONG NUMBER.'

I shook my family tree and
a bunch of nuts fell out.

HEREDITY: EVERYONE BELIEVES IN IT UNTIL THEIR CHILDREN ACT LIKE FOOLS.

Father: I don't scare easily.
Pregnant mother: All four
of our daughters will be
teenagers at the same time.

FISH AND FISHING

How do you communicate with a fish?
Drop it a line.

What did the fisherman say
to the card magician?
Take a cod, any cod.

Why did the vegan go deep-sea fishing?
Just for the halibut.

If fish lived on land, in which
country would they live?
Finland.

WHAT SWIMS IN THE SEA, CARRIES A MACHINE GUN, AND MAKES YOU AN OFFER YOU CAN'T REFUSE?

THE CODFATHER.

Give a man a fish and you feed him for a day. But teach a man to fish and you get rid of him for a whole weekend.

What is the fastest fish in the water?
A motopike.

Where do fish sleep?
In a river bed.

Two fish are in a tank. One says to the other: 'Can you drive this thing?'

WHAT IS THE DIFFERENCE BETWEEN A FISH AND A PIANO?

YOU CAN'T TUNA FISH.

Which fish can perform operations?

A sturgeon.

WHY CAN'T YOU TELL A JOKE WHILE ICE FISHING?

BECAUSE IT'LL CRACK YOU UP.

A man went into a fish shop
carrying a trout under his arm.
'Do you make fishcakes?' he asked.
'Yes, we do,' replied the fishmonger.
'Great,' said the man. 'It's his birthday.'

FLYING

What do you call it when you're
sick of being in the airport?
Terminal illness.

What do you get when you cross
an aeroplane with a magician?
A flying sorcerer.

What kind of chocolate do
they sell at the airport?
Plane chocolate.

What do you get when you
cross a snake and a plane?
A Boeing constrictor.

Why don't ducks tell jokes when they fly?
Because they would quack up.

Why can't spiders become pilots?
Because they only know how to tailspin.

What do you call a flying primate?
A hot-air baboon.

To become a pilot requires
a good altitude.

THE PROPELLER IS JUST A BIG FAN IN THE FRONT OF THE PLANE TO KEEP THE PILOT COOL. WANT PROOF? MAKE IT STOP — THEN WATCH THE PILOT BREAK OUT INTO A SWEAT.

Booking a flight, a woman told the man behind the ticket desk, 'Send one of my bags to New York, send one to Los Angeles, and send one to Miami.'
'We can't do that!' said the man.
'You did it last week!'

It was mealtime on a small airline and the flight attendant asked a passenger if he would like dinner.
'What are my choices?' he asked.
'Yes or no,' she replied.

When you're wearing a watch
on a plane, time flies.

Pilot: Evidence of leak on
right main landing gear.
Engineers: Evidence removed.

Airlines have become so cash-strapped,
they are charging me now for my
emotional baggage.

Did you hear about the pilot
who always had work?
He was great at landing a job.

'I'VE NEVER FLOWN BEFORE,' SAID THE NERVOUS OLD LADY TO THE PILOT. 'YOU WILL BRING ME DOWN SAFELY, WON'T YOU?'

'ALL I CAN SAY MA'AM,' SAID THE PILOT, 'IS THAT I'VE NEVER LEFT ANYONE UP THERE YET!'

FOOD AND DRINK

What do you call a fake noodle?
An impasta.

What does a nosey pepper do?
It gets jalapeño business!

Why don't eggs tell jokes?
They'd crack each other up.

What did the baby corn say to its mum?
'Where's my pop corn?'

WHAT DO YOU CALL CHEESE THAT ISN'T YOURS?

NACHO CHEESE!

What's red and green and
wears boxing gloves?
A fruit punch.

What do you call a cashew
in a spacesuit?
An astronut.

If a crocodile makes shoes, what
does a banana make?
Slippers.

What are twins' favourite fruit?
Pears.

What do you give to a sick lemon?
Lemon aid.

Why did the lady love to
drink hot chocolate?
Because she was a cocoa-nut.

How do you make a milk shake?
Give it a good scare.

Why don't you starve in a desert?
Because of all the 'sand which is' there.

Why shouldn't you tell a
secret on a farm?

**Because the potatoes have
eyes and the corn has ears.**

WHAT DO ELVES MAKE SANDWICHES WITH?

SHORTBREAD.

Why did the banana
go to the doctor?

Because it wasn't peeling well.

Why do the French like
to eat snails?

Because they don't like fast food.

DID YOU HEAR THE JOKE ABOUT THE PEANUT BUTTER?

I'M NOT TELLING YOU. YOU MIGHT SPREAD IT.

What's the best thing
to put into a pie?

Your teeth!

I TRIED TO GET INTO MY HOUSE THE OTHER DAY, BUT I COULDN'T. YOU KNOW WHY?

BECAUSE I HAD GNOCCHI!

What kind of girlfriend
does a potato want?
A sweet potato.

A toast to bread! For without
bread, there could be no toast.

Stop with all the bread jokes. I
don't love bread; I loaf it.

Why did the cookie cry?
**Because his mother had
been a wafer so long.**

FOOTBALL

Why do magicians make great footballers?
Because they do hat-tricks.

Why don't they build football
stadiums on the moon?
Because there's no atmosphere.

What happened when the
footballer took a corner?
He turned the pitch into a triangle.

Why did the duck get sent off the pitch?
For fowl play.

WHY SHOULD YOU NEVER INVITE A FOOTBALL PLAYER TO YOUR DINNER PARTY?

BECAUSE HE WOULD SPEND THE WHOLE TIME DRIBBLING.

James was late for school. When his teacher asked him why, James replied, 'Sorry, Miss, I was dreaming about a football match.' She looked confused and said, 'But that still doesn't explain why you're late.' He replied, 'There was extra time.'

Why should you never play football against a group of big cats?
They might be cheetahs.

Why did the chicken cross
the football pitch?
To egg on the players.

What's black and white and black
and white and black and white?
**A Newcastle fan rolling
down a hill.**

What's red, white and smiling?
**The Sunderland fan
who pushed him.**

How do you know when
it's a cup draw?

**The managers sit around
sketching crockery.**

WHAT DOES THE GOALIE LIKE TO DO WHEN HE'S HAD A BAD GAME?

HIT THE BARS.

What did the footballer's wife
say when she went to
the World Cup Final?

**The world would never
fit in that cup.**

MANAGER: THE TEAM'S NEW WINGER COST TEN MILLION. I CALL HIM OUR WONDER PLAYER.

FAN: WHY'S THAT? IS HE REALLY GOOD?

MANAGER: NO. IT'S BECAUSE WHEN I WATCH HIM PLAY I WONDER WHY I BOUGHT HIM.

After resigning from a football club, the ex-manager gave a press conference. 'And how did the crowd react?' asked one journalist. 'Were they behind you?' The ex-manager replied, 'They were right behind me, the whole lot of them, but I managed to lose them at the motorway roundabout.'

Why don't most bankers like regular football?
They prefer fiver-side.

Schoolboy: The ref sent me off.
Mum: What for?
Schoolboy: The rest of the game.

WHY DIDN'T THE SANDWICH SHOW UP TO FOOTBALL TRAINING?
BECAUSE HE WAS ONLY A SUB.

Why will an artist never
win a game of football?
Because they keep drawing.

FROGS

FROGS

What happened to the
illegally parked frog?
He got toad away.

What did the bus driver say to the frog?
Hop on.

What's a frog's favourite lawn game?
Croak-et.

How do sad frogs die?
They Kermit suicide.

What do stylish frogs wear?

Jumpsuits!

WHAT DID THE FROG ORDER AT THE BURGER BAR?

FRENCH FLIES AND A DIET CROAK.

Why did the frog say 'bark'?

He was learning a foreign language.

WHAT KIND OF SHOES DO FROGS PREFER?
OPEN TOAD SANDALS.

What do frogs drink?
Hot croako with marshmallows.

HOW DID THE TOAD DIE?
HE SIMPLY CROAKED.

What goes dot-dot-croak,
dot-dash-croak?
Morse toad.

WHAT WAS THE AMPHIBIAN'S JOB ON THE CRUISE LINER?

HE WAS THE FROGHORN.

What's green and slimy and
found at the North Pole?
A lost frog.

Why are frogs so happy?
They eat whatever bugs them.

What do you call a woman
with a frog on her head?
Lilly.

When I was younger, I dressed up as a
frog and robbed a bank. That was the
first time that I Kermit-ted a crime.

What do you get when you
cross a frog with a rabbit?
A bunny ribbit.

What do drunk toads play?
Hop-scotch.

What's green and tough?
A frog with a machine gun.

How does a frog win a gold medal?
In the long jump.

GARDENING

Why do potatoes make
good detectives?

**Because they keep
their eyes peeled.**

WHAT KIND OF SOCKS DOES A GARDENER WEAR?

GARDEN HOSE.

Knock, Knock!

Who's there?

Lettuce.

Lettuce who?

Lettuce in – it's cold out here.

What do you call two young married spiders?

Newly webs.

The best way to garden is to put on a wide-brimmed straw hat and some old clothes. And with a hoe in one hand and a cold drink in the other, tell somebody else where to dig.

Why do melons have fancy weddings?

Because they cantaloupe.

Why did the tomato turn red?

Because it saw the salad dressing.

SOMEONE KEEPS DUMPING SOIL ALL OVER MY ALLOTMENT, AND I DON'T KNOW WHO'S DOING IT. THE PLOT THICKENS.

New gardeners learn
by trowel and error.

IF ONLY I COULD GROW GREEN STUFF IN MY GARDEN LIKE I CAN IN MY FRIDGE.

Knowledge is knowing a
tomato is a fruit; wisdom is
not putting it in a fruit salad.

What does the letter 'A' have
in common with a flower?
**They both have bees
coming after them.**

WHAT DO YOU CALL IT WHEN WORMS TAKE OVER THE WORLD?
GLOBAL WORMING.

What is small, red and whispers?
A hoarse radish.

Are you a scratch player?

I sure am – every time I hit the ball I scratch my head and wonder where it went.

HOW MANY GOLFERS DOES IT TAKE TO CHANGE A LIGHT BULB?

FORE!

What's the problem with my golf game?

You're standing too close to the ball... after you've hit it.

GOLFER: I'D MOVE HEAVEN
AND EARTH TO BREAK 100
ON THIS COURSE.

CADDIE: TRY HEAVEN.
YOU'VE ALREADY MOVED
MOST OF THE EARTH.

Wife: You spend too much time thinking about golf! Do you even remember the day we got married?

Husband: Of course I do! It was the same day I sank that 45-foot putt!

THE GAME OF GOLF IS 90 PER CENT MENTAL AND 10 PER CENT MENTAL.

Why do golfers always carry a spare pair of trousers?

In case they get a hole in one.

Golfer: Hey caddie, would you wade into that pond and see if you can find my ball?

Caddie: Why?

Golfer: It's my lucky ball.

The schoolteacher was taking her first golfing lesson.

'Is the word spelt p-u-t or p-u-t-t?' she asked the instructor.

'P-u-t-t is correct,' he replied. 'Put means to place a thing where you want it. Putt means merely a vain attempt to do the same thing.'

GRANDPARENTS

A ten-year-old boy was stuck with his maths homework. 'Grandpa,' he pleaded, 'could you help me with this?'

'I could,' replied his grandfather, 'but it wouldn't be right, would it?'

'I don't suppose it would, Grandpa,' said the boy, 'but have a shot at it anyway.'

Over the holidays, some children get taken to church for a Christmas service by their grandparents. Halfway through, a grandpa leans over and whispers in his wife's ear, 'I've just let out a silent fart. What do you think I should do?' The grandma replies, 'Put a new battery in your hearing aid.'

MY GRANDMOTHER STARTED WALKING FIVE MILES A DAY WHEN SHE WAS 60. NOW SHE'S 97 YEARS OLD AND WE DON'T KNOW WHERE SHE IS.

GRANDPARENTS

A grandfather who had serious hearing problems for a number of years went to the doctor to be fitted for a hearing aid that would return his hearing to 100 per cent.

He went back for further tests a month later and the doctor said, 'Your hearing is perfect. Your family must be really pleased that you can hear again.'

To which the elderly man replied, 'Oh, I haven't told my family yet. I just sit around and listen to the conversations. I've changed my will three times!'

A grandson asked his grandad how old he was. The grandad teasingly replied, 'I'm not sure.' 'Look in your underwear, Grandpa,' he advised. 'Mine says I'm four to six.'

A grandmother was testing her granddaughter's knowledge of colours by pointing something out and asking what colour she thought it was. The little girl would answer and was always correct. At last, she headed for the door, saying, 'Grandma, I think you should try to figure out some of these colours yourself!'

WHY DID GRANDMA PUT WHEELS ON HER ROCKING CHAIR?

SHE WANTED TO ROCK AND ROLL!

HALLOWEEN

What is an Egyptian mummy's
favourite type of music?
Wrap.

What's a monster's favourite bean?
A human bean.

What do you call a witch who
lives at the beach?
A sand-witch.

Why do demons and ghouls
hang out together?
**Because demons are a
ghoul's best friend!**

Where does a ghost go
on Saturday night?

Anywhere where he can boo-gie.

WHAT DID THE SKELETON
SAY TO THE VAMPIRE?

YOU SUCK.

What do ghosts say when
something is really great?

That's so ghoul.

Why did the ghost go into the bar?
For the boos.

What is the most important subject
a witch learns in school?
Spelling.

Why did the game warden
arrest the ghost?
He didn't have a haunting license.

What happens when a ghost
gets lost in the fog?
He is mist.

Where did the goblin hit the ball?
Over the ghoul line.

Why is a ghost such a messy eater?
Because he is always a goblin.

What do you call a phantom who
gets too close to a bonfire?
A toasty ghosty.

Why didn't the skeleton
dance at the party?
He had no body to dance with.

WHY DOESN'T DRACULA MIND THE DOCTOR LOOKING AT HIS THROAT?

BECAUSE OF THE COFFIN.

What tops off a ghost's ice cream sundae?
Whipped scream.

What is a ghost's favourite kind of street?
A dead end.

What is a vampire's favourite holiday?
Fangsgiving.

What kind of make-up do ghosts wear?
Mas-scare-a.

Why are ghosts so bad at lying?
**Because you can see
right through them.**

WHAT IS A VAMPIRE'S FAVOURITE FRUIT?
A NECTARINE.

Why is a skeleton so mean?
He doesn't have a heart.

HEADLINES

HOMICIDE VICTIMS RARELY TALK TO POLICE

MOST EARTHQUAKE DAMAGE IS CAUSED BY SHAKING

FEDERAL AGENTS RAID GUN SHOP, FIND WEAPONS

ALTON ATTORNEY ACCIDENTALLY SUES HIMSELF

CITY UNSURE WHY THE SEWER SMELLS

STATE PRISONS TO REPLACE EASY-OPEN LOCKS

STOLEN PAINTING FOUND BY TREE

CHICK ACCUSES SOME OF HER MALE COLLEAGUES OF SEXISM

STATISTICS SHOW THAT TEEN PREGNANCY DROPS OFF SIGNIFICANTLY AFTER AGE 25

BUGS FLYING AROUND WITH WINGS ARE FLYING BUGS

DEAD BODY FOUND IN CEMETERY

DIANA WAS STILL ALIVE HOURS BEFORE SHE DIED

ONE-ARMED MAN APPLAUDS THE KINDNESS OF STRANGERS

WAR DIMS HOPE FOR PEACE

COLD WAVE LINKED TO TEMPERATURES

TYPHOON RIPS THROUGH CEMETERY; HUNDREDS DEAD

INCLUDE YOUR CHILDREN WHEN BAKING COOKIES

HEAVEN AND HELL

Three buddies die in a car crash, and they go to Heaven to an orientation.

They are all asked, 'When you are in your casket and friends and family are mourning over you, what would you like to hear them say about you?'

The first man says, 'I would like to hear them say that I was a great doctor of my time, and a great family man.'

The second man says, 'I would like to hear that I was a wonderful husband and schoolteacher who made a huge difference in the lives of many children.'

The last man says, 'I would like to hear them say, "Look! He's moving!"'

GOD WAS TALKING TO ONE OF HIS ANGELS. HE SAID, 'I'VE JUST CREATED A 24-HOUR PERIOD OF ALTERNATING LIGHT AND DARKNESS ON EARTH.' THE ANGEL SAID, 'WHAT ARE YOU GOING TO DO NOW?' AND GOD REPLIED, 'I THINK I'LL CALL IT A DAY.'

Did you know that Heaven and Hell are actually right next to each other? They are separated by a big chain-link fence. Well, one day Hell was having a big party and it got a little out of hand. God heard the ruckus and arrived to find his fence completely smashed by the wild partiers.

He called the Devil over and said, 'Look, Satan, you have to rebuild this fence.' Satan agreed. The next day God noticed that the Devil had completely rebuilt the fence... but it was 2 feet further into Heaven than before.

'Satan!' beckoned God. 'You have to take that fence down and put it back where it belongs!'

'Yeah? What if I don't?' replied the Devil.

'I'll sue you if I have to,' answered God.

'Sure,' laughed Satan. 'Where are you going to find a lawyer?'

HOLIDAYS

Why don't mummies go on holiday?
They're afraid to relax and unwind!

WHERE DO SHARKS GO ON HOLIDAY?
FINLAND.

What do you call six weeks
of rain in Scotland?
Summer.

WHAT DID THE PIG SAY AT THE BEACH ON A HOT SUMMER'S DAY?

I'M BACON!

What do you call a French guy in sandals?
Phillipe Phloppe.

Why did the robot go on holiday?
He needed to recharge his batteries.

Why did the gymnast put extra salt
on her food in the summer?
She wanted to do summer salts.

What does bread do on its
summer holidays?
It just loafs around.

Fred had been on a camping
trip for a few days.

'Did your tent leak?' asked
his dad when he returned.

'Only when it rained,' said Fred.

WHY DIDN'T THE ELEPHANT BUY A SUITCASE FOR HIS TRAVELS?

BECAUSE HE ALREADY HAD A TRUNK.

I'll tell you what I love doing
more than anything – trying to
pack myself in a small suitcase.
I can hardly contain myself.

HORSES

A white horse walks into a pub and asks for a whisky.

The landlord says, 'Hey, we've got a whisky named after you.'

The horse replies, 'What, George?'

Did you hear about the depressed horse?

He told a tale of whoa!

THE BUMPER BOOK OF JOKES

A poorly-looking horse limps into a bar with a bandage round his head. He orders a glass of champagne, a vintage brandy and two pints of Guinness. He downs the lot and says to the barman, 'I shouldn't really be drinking this with what I've got.'
'Why, what have you got?'
'About £2 and a carrot.'

Which side of a horse has more hair?
The outside.

BLACK BEAUTY...
WHAT A DARK HORSE.

Why did the horse cross the road?
Because somebody shouted hay!

What do you call a scary female horse?
A nightmare.

Are you a horse? Yay or neigh?

What did the horse say to the foal?
It's pasture bedtime.

HOSPITAL

Hospital regulations require a wheelchair for patients being discharged. However, while working as a student nurse, I found one elderly gentleman already dressed and sitting on the bed with a suitcase at his feet, who insisted he didn't need my help to leave the hospital.

After a chat about rules being rules, he reluctantly let me wheel him to the lift. On the way down I asked him if his wife was meeting him.

'I don't know,' he said. 'She's still upstairs in the bathroom changing out of her hospital gown.'

A man was rushed in to hospital yesterday because he swallowed a five-pound note. They are keeping him in for observation on his condition – but so far there has been no change.

Jerry was in the hospital recovering from surgery when a nurse asked him how he was feeling.
'I'm OK, but I didn't like the four-letter-word the doctor used in surgery,' he answered.
'What did he say?' asked the nurse.
'Oops!'

IAIN SPEAKS FRANTICALLY INTO THE PHONE, 'MY WIFE IS PREGNANT, AND HER CONTRACTIONS ARE ONLY TWO MINUTES APART.'

'IS THIS HER FIRST CHILD?' THE DOCTOR QUERIES.

'NO, YOU IDIOT,' SHOUTS IAIN. 'THIS IS HER HUSBAND!'

Genuine patients' charts:

On the second day the knee was better,
and on the third day it disappeared.

She is numb from her toes down.

Occasional, constant, infrequent headaches.

Discharge status: Alive but
without permission.

HOTELS

A man checks into a hotel for the first time in his life, and goes up to his room. Five minutes later he calls the front desk and says, 'You've given me a room with no exit. How do I leave?'

The person on the desk says, 'Sir, that's absurd. Have you looked for the door?'

The man says, 'Well, there's one door that leads to the bathroom. There's a second door that goes into the closet. And there's a door I haven't tried, but it has a "do not disturb" sign on it.'

A farmer, who went to a
big city to see the sights,
asked the hotel receptionist
about the times of meals.
'Breakfast is served from 7 to 11,
lunch from 12 to 3, and dinner from
6 to 8,' explained the receptionist.
'Look here,' inquired the farmer
in surprise, 'when am I going
to get time to see the city?'

Guest: Does the water always
come through the roof like that?
Hotel manager: No, sir.
Only when it rains.

A traveller pulls into a motel in America around midnight and asks the receptionist for a single room. As the clerk fills out the paperwork, the man looks around and sees a gorgeous blonde sitting in the lobby. He tells the clerk to wait while he disappears into the lobby. After a minute he comes back, with the girl on his arm.

'Fancy meeting my wife here,' he says to the clerk. 'Guess I'll need a double room for the night.'

Next morning, he comes to settle his bill, and finds the amount to be over $3,000. 'What's the meaning of this?' he yells at the clerk. 'I've only been here one night!'

'Yes,' says the clerk, 'but your wife has been here for three weeks.'

THE INTERNET

How do trees get on the internet?
They log in.

What do computers like to eat?
Chips.

What is a computer's first sign of old age?
Loss of memory.

Why did the chicken cross the web?
To get to the other site.

What kind of doctor fixes
broken websites?
A URLologist.

WHAT DO BUILDERS USE
TO MAKE WEBSITES?
COM.CRETE.

Customer: I bought this
computer yesterday and I found
a twig in the disk drive!
Employee: I'm sorry, sir, you'll have
to speak to the branch manager.

DOES YOUR MUM LIKE
SHOPPING ON THE INTERNET?
NO, THE TROLLEY KEEPS
ROLLING OFF THE COMPUTER.

Teacher: What are the four elements?
Pupil: Fire, earth, water and the internet.
Teacher: What do you mean the internet?
Pupil: Well, Mum says that whenever I'm on the net, I'm in my element.

Teacher: Don't forget to check the internet if you have trouble with your homework questions.
Pupil: It's not the questions I have trouble with – it's the answers.

Sally: My dog likes to sit down each evening and surf the net.
Joan: What an intelligent animal!
Sally: Not really – it took the cat three weeks to teach him.

KNOCK KNOCK JOKES

Knock knock!
Who's there?
Old lady.
Old lady who?
I didn't know you could yodel!

Knock knock!
Who's there?
Doris.
Doris who?
Doris locked – that's why I'm knocking!

Knock knock!
Who's there?
Police.
Police who?
Police let me in – I'm freezing out here!

KNOCK KNOCK!
WHO'S THERE?
LUKE.
LUKE WHO?
LUKE THROUGH THE WINDOW AND YOU'LL SEE!

Knock knock!
Who's there?
Pecan.
Pecan who?
Pecan someone your own size!

Knock knock!
Who's there?
Dexter.
Dexter who?
Dexter halls with boughs of holly.

Knock knock!
Who's there?
Annie.
Annie who?
Annie thing you can do, I can do better.

Knock knock!
Who's there?
Cherry.
Cherry who?
Cherry oh, see you later!

Knock knock!
Who's there?
Chester.
Chester who?
Chester minute, don't you recognise me?

Knock knock!
Who's there?
Don.
Don who?
Don mess about. Just open the door!

Knock knock!
Who's there?
Gladys.
Gladys who?
Gladys the weekend, aren't you?

Knock knock!
Who's there?
Esther.
Esther who?
Esther anything I can do for you?

Knock knock!
Who's there?
Hatch.
Hatch who?
Bless you!

Knock knock!
Who's there?
Nana.
Nana who?
Nana your business!

Knock knock!
Who's there?
Who.
Who who?
Is there an owl in there?

Knock knock!
Who's there?
Onya.
Onya who?
Onya marks, get set, go!

Knock knock!
Who's there?
Anita!
Anita who?
Anita show you something!

Knock knock!
Who's there?
Ivor.
Ivor who?
Ivor special delivery!

Knock, knock!
Who's there?
Shirley.
Shirley who?
Shirley you're tired of all these
'knock knock' jokes by now?

LAWYERS

How many lawyers does it take
to screw in a light bulb?

**Three. One to climb the ladder.
One to shake it. And one to
sue the ladder company.**

HOW MANY PERSONAL INJURY LAWYERS DOES IT TAKE TO CHANGE A LIGHT BULB?

HOW MANY CAN YOU AFFORD?

Two lawyers entered a cafe and
ordered a couple of drinks. They then
took sandwiches from their briefcases
and began to eat. Seeing this, the
angry owner went over to them and
said, 'Excuse me, but you cannot eat
your own sandwiches in here!'

Shrugging their shoulders, the
lawyers exchanged sandwiches.

A defendant isn't happy with how things are going in court, so he gives the judge a hard time:

Judge: Where do you work?
Defendant: Here and there.
Judge: What do you do for a living?
Defendant: This and that.
Judge: Take him away.
Defendant: Wait – when will I get out?
Judge: Sooner or later.

There are two kinds of lawyers: those who know the law and those who know the judge.

A lawyer dies and goes to Heaven.
'There must be some mistake,'
the lawyer argues. 'I'm too young
to die. I'm only fifty-five.'
'Fifty-five?' says Saint Peter. 'No, according
to our calculations, you're eighty-two.'
'How'd you get that?' the lawyer asks.
'We added up your time sheets.'

An investment banker decides she needs
in-house counsel, so she interviews
a young lawyer. 'Mr Peterson,' she
says. 'Would you say you're honest?'
'Honest?' replies Peterson. 'Let me tell
you something about honesty. My father
lent me $85,000 for my education, and
I paid back every penny the minute
I tried my first case.' 'Impressive.
And what sort of case was that?'
'My dad sued me for the money.'

A MAN WENT TO HIS LAWYER AND SAID, 'I WOULD LIKE TO MAKE A WILL BUT I DON'T KNOW EXACTLY HOW TO GO ABOUT IT.'

THE LAWYER SAID, 'NO PROBLEM, LEAVE IT ALL TO ME.'

THE MAN LOOKED SOMEWHAT UPSET AND SAID, 'WELL, I KNEW YOU WERE GOING TO TAKE THE BIGGEST SLICE, BUT I WOULD LIKE TO LEAVE A LITTLE TO MY CHILDREN TOO!'

LIGHT-BULB JOKES

How many psychiatrists does it
take to change a light bulb?

**Only one, but the bulb has got
to really WANT to change.**

HOW MANY ACCOUNTANTS DOES IT TAKE TO CHANGE A LIGHT BULB?

WHAT SORT OF ANSWER DID YOU HAVE IN MIND?

How many Einsteins does it take
to change a light bulb?

**That depends on the speed of the
changer, and the mass of the bulb. Or
vice versa, of course. Then it just might
be easier to leave the bulb alone and
change the room. It's all relative.**

HOW MANY AEROSPACE ENGINEERS DOES IT TAKE TO CHANGE A LIGHT BULB?

NONE. IT DOESN'T TAKE A ROCKET SCIENTIST, YOU KNOW.

How many actors does it take
to change a light bulb?

**Two. One to stand on a chair and change
it and one to say, 'I wish I was up there!'**

How many archaeologists does it
take to change a light bulb?

**Three. One to change it and two to
argue about how old the old one is.**

How many visitors to an art gallery
does it take to screw in a light bulb?

**Two. One to do it and one to say, 'Huh!
My four-year-old could've done that!'**

How many magicians does it
take to change a light bulb?

**It depends on what you
want it changed into...**

While volunteering in a soup kitchen, I hit it off with a very attractive single man. It was a relief, since my mother and I always laughed because the men to whom I was drawn were inevitably married. So, optimistic about my chances, I asked my new friend what he did for a living. He replied, 'I'm a priest.'

WHY SHOULD YOU NEVER BREAK UP WITH A GOALIE?

BECAUSE HE'S A KEEPER.

I told my girlfriend that it looked like she was drawing her eyebrows too high. She looked surprised.

WHAT DID ONE BOAT SAY
TO THE OTHER?

'ARE YOU UP FOR A
LITTLE ROW-MANCE?'

What's the difference between
love and marriage?

**Love is blind but marriage
is an eye-opener.**

WHAT DID THE GUY WITH THE BROKEN LEG SAY TO HIS NURSE?

'I'VE GOT A CRUTCH ON YOU.'

What's the difference between
love and marriage?

**Love is one long sweet dream,
and marriage is the alarm clock.**

MARRIAGE

Why is marriage like a hot bath?
**The longer you stay in,
the colder it gets.**

A man whose house had been burgled heard that the culprit had been caught. He went straight down to the police station and demanded to speak with the burglar. The copper on duty replied, 'You'll get your chance in court, sir.' To which the man pleaded, 'Please, I just want to ask him how he got in without waking my wife. I've been trying to do that for years!'

Why is marriage like a violin?
**When the sweet music's over,
the strings are still attached.**

On their fortieth wedding
anniversary, a sixty-year-old
couple were granted two wishes
by a fairy who appeared before
them. The wife wished to see the
world and 'poof', she had tickets
for a world cruise. The husband
wished for a wife thirty years
younger than him and 'poof',
he was ninety.

When a man picked his son up from
school he asked him, 'What part
did you get in the school play?'

His son replied, 'I'm going to be playing a
man who's been married for twenty years.'

The father patted him on the back
and said, 'Never mind, son, maybe
next time you'll get a speaking part.'

A man is standing in front of the mirror.
He says to his wife, 'I've got a bit of a
belly, and since we've been married
I've lost all my muscle definition.
And I think I might be going bald.'

His wife looks up and replies, 'Well, at
least there's nothing wrong with your eyes.'

A married couple were celebrating their sixtieth wedding anniversary. At the party everybody wanted to know how they had managed to stay married so long in this day and age. The husband responded, 'When we were first married we came to an agreement. I would make all the major decisions and my wife would make all the minor decisions. And in sixty years of marriage we have never needed to make a major decision.'

Why shouldn't you marry for money?
You can borrow it for less.

MUSIC

A young child says to his mother, 'Mum, when I grow up I'd like to be a musician.' She replies, 'Well honey, you know you can't do both.'

How do you make musicians complain?
Pay them.

How many folk singers does it take to change a light bulb?
Six. One to change it and five to sing about how good the old one was.

Why was the musician arrested?
He was in treble.

WHAT HAPPENS IF YOU SING COUNTRY MUSIC BACKWARDS?

YOU GET YOUR JOB AND YOUR WIFE BACK.

What do you get when you drop
a piano into a mineshaft?
A flat miner.

How are a banjo player and a
blind javelin thrower alike?
**Both command immediate
attention and cause alarm, forcing
everyone to move out of range.**

Why are violist's fingers like lightning?
They rarely strike the same spot twice.

How many guitar players does it
take to screw in a light bulb?
**Thirteen. One to do it, and
twelve to stand around and
say, 'Phhhwt! I can do that!'**

How many concertmasters does
it take to change a light bulb?
Just one, but it takes four movements.

What's the definition of a gentleman?
**Someone who knows how to play
the bagpipes, but doesn't.**

What's green and sings?
Elvis Parsley.

How does Bob Marley like his doughnuts?
Wi' jammin'.

A tourist is sightseeing in a European city. She comes upon the tomb of Beethoven, and begins reading the commemorative plaque, only to be distracted by a low scratching noise, as if something was rubbing against a piece of paper. She collars a passing native and asks what the scratching sound is. The local person replies, 'Oh, that's Beethoven. He's decomposing.'

Want to hear the joke about a staccato?
Never mind – it's too short.

NEIGHBOURS

'How's the flat you're living in in London, Jock?' asks his mother when he calls home to Aberdeen.

'It's OK,' he replies, 'but the woman next door keeps screaming and crying all night and the guy on the other side keeps banging his head on the wall.'

'Never you mind,' says his mother, 'don't you let them get to you, just ignore them.'

'Aye, that I do,' he says. 'I just keep playing my bagpipes.'

My neighbour asked if he could use my lawnmower and I told him of course he could, so long as he didn't take it out of my garden.

I just got skylights put in my place.
The woman upstairs is furious.

MY NEIGHBOURS HAVE BEEN LISTENING TO MUSIC ALL NIGHT... I LOVE MY STEREO.

If I ever win the lottery, all of my neighbours are going to be so rich!
I'm going to move to a rich neighbourhood.

My internet went down yesterday.
**I think my cheap neighbour
forgot to pay the bill.
How irresponsible.**

Three boy scouts told their
scoutmaster that they had done
their good deed for the day.
'What did you do boys?'
asked the scoutmaster.
'We helped an elderly
neighbour across the street,'
they chimed in unison.
The scoutmaster looked mystified.
'Did it take all three of you to do that?'
'Yes, it did,' said the boys.
'She didn't want to go.'

A WIFE WAS KEEPING A CLOSE WATCH ON HER NEW NEIGHBOURS. 'THEY SEEM PERFECTLY DEVOTED TO EACH OTHER,' SHE TOLD HER HUSBAND. 'HE KISSES HER EVERY TIME HE GOES OUT, AND EVEN BLOWS KISSES TO HER FROM THE WINDOW. WHY DON'T YOU DO THAT?'

'I HARDLY KNOW THE WOMAN.'

My next-door neighbour keeps racing pigeons... but the pigeons always win.

A wife went to the police station with her next-door neighbour to report that her husband was missing. The policeman asked for a description. She said, 'He's 35 years old, 6 foot 4, has dark eyes, dark wavy hair, an athletic build, weighs 185 pounds, is soft-spoken, and is good to the children.'

The next-door neighbour protested, 'Your husband is 5 foot 4, chubby, bald, has a big mouth, and is mean to your children.'

The wife replied, 'Yes, but who wants HIM back?'

PARENTS

Parenting is mostly just informing kids how many more minutes they have of something.

When Dad came home he was astonished to see Alec sitting on a horse, writing something.

'What on earth are you doing there?' he asked.

'Well, the teacher told us to write an essay on our favourite animal. That's why I'm here and that's why Susie's sitting in the goldfish bowl!'

A six-year-old boy called his mother from his friend Charlie's house and confessed he had broken a lamp when he threw a football in their living room.

'But, Mum,' he said, brightening, 'you don't have to worry about buying another one. Charlie's mother said it was irreplaceable.'

Big Brother: 'That planet over there is Mars.'
Little Brother: 'Then that other one must be Pa's.'

George knocked on the door of his friend's house. When his friend's mother answered he asked, 'Can Albert come out to play?'

'No,' said the mother, 'it's too cold.'

'Well, then,' said George, 'can his football come out to play?'

Two kids are talking to each other. One says, 'I'm really worried. My dad works twelve hours a day to give me a nice home and good food. My mum spends the whole day cleaning and cooking for me. I'm worried sick!'

The other kid says, 'What have you got to worry about? Sounds to me like you've got it made!'

The first kid says, 'What if they try to escape?'

PARTIES

Why did the mushroom get
invited to all the parties?
Because he's a fungi.

WHY DID THE FUNGI LEAVE THE PARTY?
THERE WASN'T MUSHROOM.

Why wasn't there any food left
after the monster party?
Because everyone was a goblin.

What does an actuary do
to liven up a party?
He invites an accountant.

A husband and wife were at a
party chatting with some friends
when the subject of marriage
counselling came up. 'Oh, we'll
never need that. My wife and I
have a great relationship,' the
husband explained. 'She studied
communications at university
and I studied theatre.' He
continued, 'She communicates
well and I act like I'm listening.'

PARTIES

At a country club party a young man was introduced to an attractive girl. He immediately began paying her court and flattering her. The girl liked the young man, but she was taken aback by his fast and ardent pitch. She was amazed when, after 30 minutes, he seriously proposed marriage.

'Look,' she reacted. 'We only met a half hour ago. How can you be so sure? We know nothing about each other.'

'You're wrong,' the young man replied. 'For the past five years I've been working in the bank where your father has his account.'

At a dinner party, one of the guests, an obnoxiously loud young man, tried to make clever remarks about everyone and everything. When he was served a piece of meat, he picked it up with his fork, held it up and smirked, 'Is this pig?' Another guest, sitting opposite, asked quietly: 'Which end of the fork are you referring to?'

A man tried to gatecrash a fancy dress party at a bar. He was dressed as a pair of jump leads. After initially turning the man away, the bouncer on the door relented, saying, 'OK, you can enter, but just don't start anything.'

'I'M GIVING A "SURPRISED" BIRTHDAY PARTY FOR YOU.'

'WHAT'S THAT?'

'THAT'S WHERE I INVITE A BUNCH OF YOUR FRIENDS, AND IF ANY OF THEM COME, I'LL BE SURPRISED!'

RESTAURANTS

Did you hear about the new restaurant on the moon?
Great food but no atmosphere.

WHICH *STAR WARS* CHARACTER WORKS AT A RESTAURANT?
DARTH WAITER.

Diner: Are you sure this place is hygienic?

Manager: Yes, sir. You could eat off the floor.

Diner: That's the problem. It looks as if somebody has!

Why was the restaurant called 'Out of this World'?

Because it was full of Unidentified Frying Objects.

THERE WAS AN AWFUL FIGHT AT THE SEAFOOD RESTAURANT. FOUR FISH GOT BATTERED!

My wife and I went for a meal the other night and I surprised everyone there by ordering in French.

It was an Italian restaurant.

My wife and I went for a meal the other night and I said to the waiter, 'This chicken is stone cold.' 'It should be,' he replied, 'it has been dead for over a week.'

I went to a restaurant last week and just as my soup arrived, I needed the toilet. To make sure that nobody tampered with it, I wrote on my napkin: 'I have spat in this soup'. On my return I noticed that the waiter had written on the napkin: 'That's OK, so have I.'

A waiter brought a customer the steak she ordered with his thumb pressing down on the meat.

The customer was furious. 'What are you doing touching my steak like that?'

'Well, madam,' replied the waiter, 'you wouldn't want it falling on the floor again, would you?'

SCHOOL

After noticing a child in her class pulling faces, a primary school teacher took the troublemaker aside and said, 'When I was little my mummy told me if I pulled faces the wind would change and it would get stuck that way.'

The naughty boy replied, 'Well, Miss, you can't say you weren't warned.'

Katie was late for school every day, so one morning her teacher asked her why.

'Because of the sign,' Katie said.

'What sign?' replied her teacher.

'The sign that says, "School ahead, go slow".'

Teacher: Do you have trouble making decisions?
Pupil: Well... yes and no.

Why did the teacher wear sunglasses to work?
Because his class was so bright.

What do opticians and teachers have in common?
They both test pupils.

Why isn't whispering permitted in class?
Because you're not aloud.

WHY DID THE STUDENT SAY HIS MARKS WERE 'UNDERWATER'?

BECAUSE THEY WERE BELOW C LEVEL.

Teacher: Which two days of the week start with the letter 't'?
Pupil: Today and tomorrow.

WHY DID THE STUDENT WRITE ON HIS TOES IN CLASS?
HE WAS TRYING TO THINK ON HIS FEET.

Teacher: Who gave you that black eye, Callum?
Callum: No one gave it to me, sir – I fought really hard for it.

Pupil: Sir, my dog ate my homework.

Teacher: And where's your dog now?

Pupil: He's at the vet's – he doesn't like maths either.

A teacher was struggling to teach arithmetic to a young boy. She asked him, 'If you reached into your right pocket and found a pound, and reached into your left pocket and found a five-pound note, what would you have?'

The boy thought the matter over and replied: 'Someone else's shorts, Miss.'

DID YOU HEAR ABOUT THE SCHOOLBOY WHO PUT CLEAN SOCKS ON EVERY DAY?

BY FRIDAY HE COULDN'T GET HIS SHOES ON.

A teacher was taking his first class at a new school. After introducing himself he announced, 'Stand up if you think you're stupid.' Nobody moved, and then after a minute, one pupil stood up. 'So you think you're an idiot, then?' said the teacher. 'No,' replied the pupil, 'I just didn't want you standing up all on your own.'

Teacher: Whenever I ask you a question, I want you to answer altogether. What is nine times four?
Class: Altogether!

Teacher: Can anyone use the word 'fascinate' in a sentence?

Pupil: My dad bought a new shirt with nine buttons, but he's so fat he was only able to fasten eight.

Pupil: I don't think I deserved zero for this exam.

Teacher: Nor do I. But I couldn't give you any lower.

WHY DID THE SCHOOLTEACHER MARRY THE CARETAKER? HE SWEPT HER OFF HER FEET.

Why did the schoolgirl only wear one glove?

Because on the weather forecast it said it might be warm, but on the other hand it could be cooler.

In an exam room the teacher snapped at one pupil, 'Oliver, I hope I didn't just see you looking at Ella's test paper?'

Oliver replied, 'I hope you didn't see me too.'

Lucy: Miss, can I go to the toilet?
Teacher: Lucy, may I go to the toilet?
Lucy: I asked first!

Mother: Why was your exam score so low last week?

Son: Absence.

Mother: What, you missed the exam?

Son: No, but the girl who sits next to me did.

Teacher: Francis, conjugate the verb 'to walk' in the simple present tense.

Francis: I walk... um... You walk...

Teacher: Quicker please, Francis.

Francis: I jog... You jog...

Pupil: What's the date today?

Examiner: That's not important. Get on with the test.

Pupil: But sir, I want to get something right.

CHILD: MY MUSIC TEACHER SAID MY SINGING WAS OUT OF THIS WORLD.

MUM: REALLY?

CHILD: WELL, SHE SAID IT WAS 'UNEARTHLY'.

Teacher: What did Henry VIII do when he came to the throne?

Pupil: He sat on it.

A teacher arrived late to class and saw an unflattering caricature of himself on the blackboard. Turning to the class he asked, 'Who is responsible for this grossness?' Sniggering, the class joker replied, 'Well, I really can't be sure, but I blame the parents.'

Teacher: How many seconds are there in a year?

Pupil: Twelve! January the 2nd, February the 2nd...

A son told his father he couldn't go to school because he didn't feel very well. 'Where don't you feel very well?' his father asked. 'In school,' the boy replied.

WHY COULDN'T THE STUDENT DIVIDE BY TWO?

SHE DIDN'T KNOW THE HALF OF IT.

Teacher: Where in England is Felixstowe?
Pupil: On the end of Felix's foot.

SCIENCE

What did the biologist wear
on his first date?
Designer genes.

Old chemistry teachers never die.
They just fail to react.

What did the receiver say
to the radio wave?
Ouch! That megahertz.

Advice to a young researcher: if at first
you succeed, try to hide your surprise.

A photon checks into a hotel and is asked if he needs any help with his luggage. The photon says, 'No thanks, I'm travelling light.'

What did the male magnet say to the female magnet?

From the back, I thought you were repulsive. However, after seeing you from the front, I find you really quite attractive.

A NEUTRON WALKED INTO A BAR AND ASKED, 'HOW MUCH IS A GIN AND TONIC?' THE BARTENDER SMILED AND REPLIED, 'FOR YOU, NO CHARGE.'

What is the name of the first electricity detective?
Sherlock Ohms

What's the difference between a dog and a marine biologist?
One wags a tail and the other tags a whale.

Where does bad light end up?
In a prism.

What did one quantum physicist say when he started to fight another quantum physicist?
Let me atom!

Have you heard about the
chemist who was reading a
book about helium?

He just couldn't put it down.

WHY DO CHEMISTS LIKE NITRATES?
BECAUSE THEY'RE CHEAPER THAN DAY RATES.

What do you do with
a sick chemist?

**If you can't helium, and you
can't curium, you might as
well barium.**

If the Silver Surfer and Iron Man team up, then they'd be alloys.

What did one ion say to the other ion? **I've got my ion you.**

Organic chemistry is difficult. Those who study it have alkynes of trouble.

Don't trust atoms – they make up everything.

SLEEP

Did you hear about the man
who plugged his electric
blanket into the toaster?

**He kept popping out
of bed all night.**

WHAT'S THE BEST ADVICE
TO GIVE A WORM?

SLEEP LATE!

Why did the idiot take a tape
measure to bed with him?

To see how long he slept.

'I DON'T THINK MY MUM
KNOWS MUCH ABOUT CHILDREN.'
'WHY DO YOU SAY THAT?'
'BECAUSE SHE ALWAYS PUTS ME TO BED
WHEN I AM WIDE AWAKE AND GETS
ME UP WHEN I AM SLEEPY.'

A teacher is someone who
talks in our sleep.

Why couldn't Dracula's wife get to sleep?
Because of his coffin.

Sleeping comes so naturally to me,
I could do it with my eyes closed.

I do ten sit-ups every morning. It might
not sound like much, but there are only so
many times you can hit the snooze button.

SPACE

What is a spaceman's favourite chocolate?
A Mars bar.

Why did the sun go to school?
To get brighter.

How do you know when the moon
has had enough to eat?
When it's full.

What do you call a tick on the moon?
A lunar-tick.

What kind of music do planets sing?
Neptunes!

What's a light-year?
**The same as a regular year,
but with fewer calories.**

Why did the cow go in the spaceship?
It wanted to see the moooooon.

What do planets like to read?
Comet books!

WHAT DID THE ALIEN
SAY TO THE GARDEN?
TAKE ME TO YOUR WEEDER!

Why don't aliens eat clowns?
Because they taste funny!

WHAT IS AN ASTRONAUT'S FAVOURITE KEY ON THE KEYBOARD?
THE SPACE BAR.

Where would an astronaut park his spaceship?
Beside a parking meteor.

What do aliens on the metric system say?
Take me to your litre.

Why does a moon rock taste
better than an earth rock?
It's a little meteor.

What did the alien say when
he was out of room?
I'm all spaced out.

What did the alien say to the cat?
Take me to your litter.

SWIMMING

How do swimmers clean themselves?
They wash up on shore.

Why can male elephants swim
whenever they want?
They always have trunks with them.

Why should you never swim
on a full stomach?
Because it's easier to swim in water.

What kind of dive are infantry men best at?
Cannon-ball.

HOW DO PEOPLE SWIMMING IN THE OCEAN SAY 'HI' TO EACH OTHER?

THEY WAVE.

What stroke do sheep enjoy doing?
The baaaackstroke!

Which direction does a chicken
swim around a swimming pool?
Cluck-wise.

What do a dentist and a swimming
coach have in common?
They both use drills.

What kind of exercises are
best for a swimmer?
Pool-ups.

Where do zombies like to go swimming?
The Dead Sea.

What race is never run?
A swimming race.

What kind of fish can't swim?
A dead one.

What kind of stroke can you use on toast?
Butter-fly.

TELEVISION

Jane: I'd love to be a TV actress.
Harry: Break a leg!
Jane: What? Why?
Harry: Then you'd be in
a cast for weeks.

What kind of TV do you find
inside a haunted house?
A wide scream TV.

TWO TELEVISION AERIALS
MET ON A ROOFTOP, FELL IN
LOVE AND GOT MARRIED.
THE CEREMONY WAS AWFUL,
BUT THE RECEPTION
WAS EXCELLENT.

Neighbour: Haven't I
seen you on TV?
Actor: Well, I do appear, on and off,
you know. How do you like me?
Neighbour: Off.

WHAT IS THE CAT'S FAVOURITE TV PROGRAMME?

THE EVENING MEWS.

Why does a chicken watch TV?
For hentertainment!

What is a dolphin's
favourite TV show?
Whale of Fortune.

DO YOU EVEN HAVE FRIENDS?
YEP, ALL TEN SERIES!

What is a cat's favourite TV show?
Miami Mice.

Two men were watching a Western on television. As the hero rode on horseback towards a cliff edge, one of the men said, 'I bet you fifty quid he goes over the cliff.'

'You're on,' said the other man.

The hero rode straight over the cliff.

As the second man handed over the money, the first man looked at it and said, 'You know, I feel a bit guilty about winning this because I've seen the film before.'

'So have I,' said the second man. 'But I didn't think he'd be stupid enough to make the same mistake twice.'

TENNIS

What do you call a girl standing in
the middle of a tennis court?
Annette.

Why are fish never good tennis players?
They don't like getting close to the net.

How many tennis players does it
take to change a light bulb?
What do you mean it was out – it was in!

What did one tennis ball say
to the other tennis ball?
'See you round...'

Why should you never fall in
love with a tennis player?
To them, 'Love' means nothing.

What can you serve but not eat?
A tennis ball.

What did the tennis ball say when it got hit?
Who's making all the racquet?

My tennis opponent was not
happy with my serve.
He kept returning it.

WHAT TIME DOES ANDY MURRAY GO TO BED?

TENNISH.

Two sardines were big tennis
fans. 'Let's go to Wimbledon
this year,' said one.
'How would we get there?'
asked the other.
'On the London
Underground, of course.'
'What, and get packed
in like commuters?'

It feels great to hit the ball
again. It spin a long time.

An orange and an apple signed up for a tournament. No one was surprised to find out they were both seeded.

TENNIS IS A LOT LIKE WAITING TABLES. THE MOST IMPORTANT THING TO GET RIGHT IS THE FIRST SERVE.

Two tennis racquets started dating. Unfortunately, one was stringing the other along without any intention of tying the knot.

379

I keep an alarm clock in the back window of my car. I'm always ahead of my time.

The clock was still hungry, so it went back four seconds.

I was going to look for my missing watch, but I could never find the time.

What if you hit your alarm clock one morning and it hit you back... that would be alarming.

WHAT DID THE LEANING TOWER OF PISA SAY TO BIG BEN?

IF YOU'VE GOT THE TIME, I'VE GOT THE INCLINATION.

The conceited watch was a bit clocky.

When do clocks die?
When their time is up.

What time is it when you sit on a pin?
Spring time.

Why did the man put a
clock under his desk?
He wanted to work overtime.

TIME

A man had been driving all night and by morning was still far from his destination. He decided to stop at the next city he came to, and park somewhere quiet so he could get an hour or two of sleep. As luck would have it, the quiet place he chose happened to be on one of the city's major jogging routes.

No sooner had he settled back to snooze when there came a knocking on his window. He looked out and saw a jogger running on the spot. 'Excuse me, sir,' the jogger said, 'do you have the time?' The man looked at the car clock and answered, '8:25'.

Now the man could see other joggers passing by and he knew it was only a matter of time before another one disturbed him. To avoid the problem, he got out a pen and paper and put a sign in his window saying, 'I do not know the time!'

Once again he settled back to sleep. He was just dozing off when there was another knock on the window. 'Sir, sir? It's 8:45!'

Why couldn't the clock
be kept in jail?
**Because time was
always running out.**

IF TIME IS MONEY, ARE ATMS TIME MACHINES?

Why did the girl sit on her watch?
She wanted to be on time.

'I hope you're not one of those boys who sits and watches the school clock,' said the headteacher to a new boy.

'No, Miss. I've got a digital watch that bleeps at three-fifteen.'

TIME FLIES LIKE AN ARROW, BUT FRUIT FLIES LIKE A BANANA.

Ever tried eating a clock? It's very time-consuming.

TOILET HUMOUR

While waiting at the doctor's surgery, a man lets rip a really loud fart. Trying to look nonchalant he turns to the woman next to him as if nothing has happened. 'Do you have a copy of today's paper I could borrow?' he asks. 'No,' she replies, 'but if you put your hand out of the window you can rip some leaves off that bush.'

Did you hear about the
blind skunk?

He's dating a fart.

A famous pirate captain had a ritual that whenever battle looked imminent, he would change into his red shirt. One day his cabin boy asked him why he did this. 'It's in case I get shot,' he replied, 'I don't want my men to see the blood and get worried.' The cabin boy nodded, and then turned to see another pirate crew, sabres raised, boarding their ship. Suddenly the nervous captain whimpered, 'Fetch me my brown trousers.'

Two flies were sitting on a dog poo. One farted and the other one turned to him and snapped, 'Do you mind? Can't you see I'm eating?'

WHY DID THE CANTANKEROUS OLD MAN TAKE TOILET PAPER TO THE PARTY WITH HIM?

BECAUSE HE WAS A PARTY POOPER.

A woman goes to see the doctor because she can't stop farting. 'It's not a huge problem because they don't smell or make a noise, but I just want them to stop. Even though you haven't noticed, I have already farted a few times in this office. Can you prescribe me something?' Looking pained, the doctor begins writing out a prescription. 'I'm prescribing some decongestants for your nose,' he says, 'and referring you for a hearing test.'

What did Mr Spock
find in the toilet?
The captain's log.

TOILET HUMOUR

An old man and his wife have gone to bed. After lying there a few minutes, the old man farts and says, 'Five points.'

His wife rolls over and says, 'What in the world was that?'

The old man replies, 'It's fart rugby.'

A few minutes later the wife lets one go and says, 'That's a try! Now we're even.'

After about five minutes the old man farts again and says, 'Try! I'm ahead 10 to 5.'

Not to be outdone the wife rips another one and says, 'Try – tie score.'

Five seconds go by and she lets out a squeaker and says, 'That's a conversion: I lead 12 to 10.'

Realising a defeat would be totally unacceptable, the old man gives it everything he has but instead of farting he poops the bed.

The wife looks over and says, 'What was that?'

The old man replies, 'Half-time, switch sides.'

WEDDINGS

The bride weeps, the bridesmaids cry
– even the wedding cake is in tiers.

The vicar at a wedding noticed that the bride was in great distress so he asked her what was wrong. She replied that she was nervous and afraid she would not remember what to do. He told her that she only needed to remember three things. First, the aisle, because that is what you'll be walking down. Secondly, the altar, because that is where you are going. Finally, remember hymn because that is a type of song we will sing during the service. While the bride was walking to the wedding march, family and friends of the groom were horrified to hear her repeating these three words: aisle, altar, hymn... aisle, altar, hymn...

THEY MARRIED FOR
BETTER OR FOR WORSE:
HE COULDN'T HAVE DONE
BETTER, AND SHE COULDN'T
HAVE DONE WORSE.

During the rehearsal for his wedding, the groom took the priest to one side and said, 'I'll give you £100 if you change my wedding vows. When you reach the part where I promise to love, honour and obey and "forsaking all others, be faithful to her for ever", I want you to leave that bit out.' The priest duly accepted the £100.

At the ceremony a few days later, the priest got to the groom's vows and said, 'Will you promise to obey her every command and wish, serve her breakfast in bed every morning, and swear that you will never look at another woman again?'

The groom was stunned. 'I thought we had a deal,' he hissed.

'Yes,' whispered the priest, pressing the £100 into the groom's hand. 'But the bride made me a better offer.'

At a wedding ceremony, the vicar asked if anyone had anything to say concerning the union of the bride and groom. It was their time to stand up and talk, or forever hold their peace. The moment of utter silence was broken by a young beautiful woman carrying a child. She started slowly walking toward the vicar. Everything quickly turned to chaos. The bride slapped the groom. The groom's mother fainted. The groomsmen started giving each other looks and wondering how best to help save the situation.

The vicar asked the woman, 'Can you tell us why you came forward? What do you have to say?'

The woman replied, 'I can't hear from right down the back.'

WHY DID THE CHICKEN...?

Why did the chicken
cross the road?

Don't ask me – ask the chicken!

WHY DID THE CHICKEN RUN ACROSS THE ROAD?

THERE WAS A CAR COMING.

Why did the chicken cross
the road halfway?

She wanted to lay it on the line.

WHY DID THE CHICKEN...?

Why did the rubber chicken
cross the road?
She wanted to stretch her legs.

Why did the Roman chicken
cross the road in a rush?
She was afraid someone would Caesar.

Why didn't the chicken
skeleton cross the road?
Because she was gutless.

Why did the sheep cross the road?
**To get to the baa-baa
shop for a haircut.**

WHY DID THE ROOSTER CROSS THE ROAD?

TO COCK-A-DOODLE-DOO SOMETHING.

Why did the duck cross the road?
Because the chicken needed a day off.

Why did the chewing gum cross the road?
Because it was stuck to the chicken's foot.

Why did the dinosaur cross the road?
Because chickens hadn't evolved yet.

Why didn't the skeleton cross the road?
Because he had no body to go with.

Why did the cow cross the road?
To get to the udder side.

WHY DID THE FISH CROSS THE SEA?
TO GET TO THE OTHER TIDE.

Why did the chicken cross the
road, roll in a muddy puddle
and cross the road again?
**Because she was a dirty
double-crosser.**

Why did the horse cross the road?
To reach his neigh-bourhood.

Why did the elephant cross the road?
To prove he wasn't chicken.

Why did the chicken cross the playground?
To get to the other slide.

Why did the dirty chicken cross the road?
For some fowl purpose.

ZOOS

Kevin: I was at the zoo last week.
Sophie: Really? Which
cage were you in?

Caller: Finally! I got through! I've
been trying to call the zoo for hours!
Zookeeper: Yes, all our lions
were busy!

Mary: You don't see many
reindeer in zoos, do you?
Dave: No. They can't
afford the admission.

HOW DO YOU FANCY A TRIP TO THE ZOO?

SURE! ALPACA MY BAGS FOR THE TRIP!

One day a zookeeper noticed that the orangutan was reading two books: the Bible and Darwin's *Origin of Species*. In surprise, he asked the ape, 'Why are you reading both those books'?
'Well,' said the orangutan, 'I just wanted to know if I was my brother's keeper or my keeper's brother.'

Five thousand hares have escaped from the zoo.
Police are combing the area.

ZOOS

One day a man was walking through his local park when he came across a penguin. Thinking the small aquatic animal could be someone's pet, out for its daily walk, the man looked around to see if anyone was nearby, but saw no one.

Unwilling to leave the penguin alone in the park, the man held out his hand, which the penguin obligingly took hold of and the pair set off together towards the park gate. Moments later, a policeman walked through the gate and upon spotting the unusual pair, called out 'Where did you find that penguin sir?'

'Just up the pathway there, officer. He was left all alone, you see, but now I'm not sure where to take him,' replied the charitable man.

This warmed the policeman's heart, and he decided to give the man directions to the local zoo. The man, with a sigh of relief, replied, 'We'll go there right away, officer. Thank you so much for the suggestion.'

The next day, the same police officer was entering the same park when he happened upon the same man sitting on the grass and, low and behold, the same penguin was sat right next to him.

The disgruntled policeman walked over to where the man was sitting and exclaimed, 'I thought you were taking that penguin to the zoo?'

'Why yes, officer, and what an excellent day we had! We'll be going to the circus tomorrow!'

Did you hear about the new
bamboo trees at the zoo?

It was panda-monium out there.

I WENT TO A ZOO ONCE — ALL THEY HAD WAS A DOG.

IT WAS A SHIH TZU.

What do you do with a blue whale?

You cheer him up, of course.

The BUMPER B⚽OK of SPORTING WIT

Richard Benson

THE BUMPER BOOK OF SPORTING WIT
Richard Benson

978-1-84953-917-3

£9.99

Hardback

I threw the kitchen sink at him but he went to the bathroom and got his tub.
Andy Roddick on Roger Federer

When I lost my decathlon world record I took it like a man. I only cried for ten hours.
Daley Thompson

I've seen George Foreman shadow boxing and the shadow won.
Muhammad Ali

Win, lose or draw, players and fans always have something to say about it. Packed to the rafters with the best quips and quotes from across the world of sport, this massive collection will keep you smiling in the stands even when you're smarting from the scoreline.

THE LITTLE
BOOK OF
CHEESE
JOKES

Jake Harris

THE LITTLE BOOK OF CHEESE JOKES
Jake Harris

978-1-84953-859-6

£5.99

Paperback

What do you call cheese that isn't yours?
Nacho cheese!

Who says cheesy jokes are a bad thing?
Not us! With this outrageously ripe selection
of gags, you'll be delighting your friends
all the way to the deli counter. Whether
you're in need of a pungent pun or a
holey howler, *The Little Book of Cheese*
Jokes offers a full smorgasbord – from the
downright immature to the truly vintage.

If you're interested in finding out more about our books, find us on Facebook at **Summersdale Publishers** and follow us on Twitter at **@Summersdale**.

www.summersdale.com